Colophon

©Mathias Jansson (2015)
"The Pioneers of Game Art: From ArsDoom to SimBee"
ISBN: 978-91-86915-18-6
Published by:

"jag behöver inget förlag"
c/o Mathias Jansson
Tvärvägen 23
232 52 Åkarp
SWEDEN
http://mathiasjansson72.blogspot.se/
Print: Lulu.com

All interviews have previously been published at Gamescenes.org 2009-2012.

Foreword

It all started in 2005 when my interest for Game Art awoke. There was not much written about the topic at this time and one question interested me more than others. How did it all start? When and how did videogames became a part of the art scene? I therefore started to interview artists, critics and curators to find an answer. My interviews were first published on the blog Gamescene.org during 2009-2012. Together they create an historic mosaic about an excing period in contemporary art and is now for the first time collected in a book.

Thanks

First of all I want to thank all the artists, critics and curators that have taken time to answer my questions. I know many of you were very busy but still you have taking the time to formulate exciting and detailed answers to the questions.

Special Thanks to Matteo Bittanti editor of Gamescene.org who from the beginning supported the concept with a series of interviews with artists working with Game Art.

Content

First Museum Shooters (essay) 5

Daniel Botz: The demoscene as Game Art's prehistory 14

Orhan Kipcak: "ArsDoom" (1995) 18

Tobias Bernstrup & Palle Torsson: "Museum Meltdown" (1996) ..23

Antonio Riello: "Italiani Brava Gente" (1996) 26

Konrad Becker: "Synreal: The Unreal Modification" (1998) 30

Anne-Marie Schleiner: "Cracking the Maze" (1999) 33

Martin Berghammer: "RELOAD" (1995) 38

Tilman Baumgärtel: "Computergames by Artist" (2003) 42

Sylvia Eckermann: "Hotel Synthifornia" (1998) 47

Josephine Starrs: "Bio Tek Kitchen" (1999) 51

Margarete Jahrmann: "Synreal exhibition" (1999) 54

Robert Nideffer: "The Tomb Raider Patch" (1999) 58

Carlo Zanni: "Average Shoeveler" (2004) 63

Joan Leandre: "retroYou" (1999-2004) 68

Julian Oliver: QTHOTH (1998-1999) 74

Joseph Delappe: "Howl" (2001) 79

Stephen Honegger: "Container" (2002) 84

Eddo Stern: "Vietnam Romance" (2003) 87

Axel Stockburger: "Tokyo Arcade Warriors" (2003) 92

Andy Clarke and Grethe Mitchell: Game Art Criticism 101

Brody Condon: "Adam Killer" (1999) 106

Suzanne Treister: "Videogame paintings" (1988-) 110

Mauro Ceolin: Emblems and Landscapes 118

Chad Chatterton: "Acmipark" (2001-2002)..............................122

John Paul Bichard: "The White Room" (2004), ...127

Rosemarie Fiore: "Arcade Game Photographs" (1980)...............133

Katherine Isbister: "SIMBEE" (2004)..135

Ben Chang: "Philosopher DeathMatch" (2006) 138

Antoinette LaFarge: "Plaintext Players" (1994).........................144

Arne-Kjell Vikhagen: "Veøy" (2006) 152

Steve Manthorp: "Shooting Gallery" (2003)..............................155

First Museum Shooters

In the Beginning was Doom

When the small company id Software in Texas, USA, 1993 released the videogame *Doom* few would have guessed that this game would change the entire game industry, and even fewer would have guessed which impact *Doom* would have on the art world. Until 1990 most videogames were played in a 2D environment in which you controlled a character or vehicle through a landscape, as in videogames as *Super Mario Bros, Pac Man or Space Invaders*. In the early 90's the First-Person Shooter genre (FPS) got its breakthrough with titles such as *Wolfenstein 3D* (1992) and *Doom* (1993) both published by id Software. The big difference with these games was that they took place in a 3D world that was generated in real time and they were played in first person (First Person Shooter). The player didn't control a character on the screen, he was the main character in the game and saw the whole game from first person view which mostly consisted of looking straight down at a loaded gun.

Already at the launch of *Wolfenstein 3D*, id Software had noticed that the players tried to build their own levels to the game and when they released *Doom* the following year, they did what they could to make it easier for the player to modify the game. They separated audio, video and music from the game and put them in WAD files (Where's All the Data?)[1] Both founder of id Software, John Romero and John Carmack, had begun there career by hacking and altering others' games and now they wanted to give something back to the gaming community and create something that gave extra value to the new game. In retrospect it is clear that this was a wise decision. Doom sold over four million copies and was long in the charts of the world's best selling computer games. The

---

[1] p.166 "Masters of Doom: How two guys created an empire and transformed pop culture" by David Kushner (Random House, 2003)

videogame *Doom* did not only created a whole new way to experience a videogame but also the conditions for a whole new art form.

The FPS genre evolved rapidly over the next few years with titles such as *Doom II* (1994), *Quake* (1996), *Unreal* (1998) and *Half-Life* (1998). Powerful new graphics engine made it possible to render even more detailed and sophisticated 3D environments. Among the new games were also new special tools that made it possible for players, to modify and extend the game by building their own levels, characters, weapons, etc. Through the Internet, which at this time began to connect players around the world, there were easy ways to spread the new modifications to other gamers. Suddenly there were a lot of new mods (modifications) to well-known game titles as *Doom, Quake and Half-Life*, which both extended the life of the games and created a growing subculture and community around them. It was in this environment a whole new generation of artists grew up with videogames and they soon began experimenting with the game tools to se how they could be used in artistic contexts.

The artist-as-gamer
The breakthrough for artistic modifications of videogames can be dated to 1995 when the Austrian artist Orhan Kipcak created *Arsdoom* to the media festival Ars Electronica in Linz, Austria.[2] *Arsdoom* consisted of an entirely new level for the game *Doom II* (1994). The level was a virtual copy of the exhibition hall in Brucknerhaus. In the virtual exhibition hall the player could found artworks of artists as Peter Weibel, Seiichi Guruya, Manfred Wolff-Plottegg, Sabine Bitter and others. The exhibiting artists were also the enemies in the game and could be killed by the player by using weapons as his fists, brushes, wooden cross and the traditional chain saw from the original *Doom* game. Except beating and killing the artists the player could also destroy the exhibited art and create

---

[2] "Mythos Information: Welcome to the Wired World, Ars Electronica 1995" ed. Karl Gerbel, Peter Weibel, (Springer Verlag, Wien, New York, 1995).

his own art. In the game the player could pick up objects from different artists as Herman Nitsch blood, with which he could spray the walls, or use Arnulf Rainer pens to draw on the artworks. There was also a feature that made it possible to turn all the artwork upside down in a style reminiscent of George Baselitz's art.[3]

Arsdoom represents a milestone in the videogame-inspired art and marks in many ways a new approach between art and audience. The audience is no longer passive consumers, but active arts producers who have control over the exhibition with full rights to destroy the works of art and shoot the artists. The concept of Arsdoom has many of the characteristic features that define artistic computer game modification. First, this type of art requires a certain habit of playing videogames from the visitors, second, it is expected that the visitor is active and interactive in order to experience the artwork. If the visitors do not play or get involved there will be no work of art. In *Arsdoom* there are also a fusion between popular culture (video games) and high culture (the established art world). Often this fusion is a bloody clash when the violent aesthetics from videogames are confronted with the rules of "not to touch the art" in the exhibition space. In art works as Arsdoom the visitors/players has every opportunity to experience the art exhibition without the normal conventions and limitations.

First Museum Shooters
It took not long before other artists started to create their own levels to popular videogames. Palle Torsson and Tobias Bernstrup were still students when they in November 1996, were invited to the Nordic biennial *The Scream: Borealis 8* at Arken, Museum of Modern Art near Copenhagen.[4] Their contribution to the exhibition was a videogame which they called *Museum Meltdown*.

---

[3] "Interview: Orhan Kipcak (ArsDoom, ArsDoom II) (1995-2005)" by Mathias Jansson Link: http://www.gamescenes.org/2009/11/interview-orphan-kipcak-arsdoom-arsdoom-ii-1995.html
[4] "The scream : Borealis 8 : Nordic fine arts 1995-96" by Kim Levin etc, (Arken Museum of Modern Art, Ishøj, 1996).

With help of the videogame *Duke Nukem* Torsson and Bernstrup recreated the architecture from the Art Museum Arken and let the visitors as in *Arsdoom*, take control over the exhibition hall where they could shoot down enemies of various kinds and destroy the works of art.[5] *Museum Meltdown* got two successors. 1997 Torsson and Bernstrup made a version of the Contemporary Art Center in Vilnius and in 1999 a new version of *Museum Meltdown* was showed at Moderna Museet in Stockholm. In the press release from the Moderna Musset exhibition the artists writes:

"Museum Meltdown is a virtual reorganization of the Museum of Modern Art and is based on the video game Half-Life. The game's logic can be displaced as well as all living art become objects for the player's destructive desires. Museum with the task of conveying / preserve our cultural heritage here is a scene of violence and destruction."[6]

In 1999 RELOAD Shift eV Gallery in Berlin arranged an exhibition with the artists Florian Muser and Imre Oswald, who exhibited a reconstruction of the Hamburger Kunsthalle created with help of the videogame *Quake*.[7] As in the previous examples, the artists created a virtual architecture of a real exhibition hall and let the visitors take a walk in the galleries armed to the teeth so they can defend themselves against enemies sneaking up around the corner and disrupting the experience of art. *Arsdoom, Museum Meltdown*, and other similar works can be categorized in a special genre called

---

[5] "Interview: Tobias Bernstrup and Palle Torsson, "Museum Meltdown" (1996)" by Mathias Jansson Link:
http://www.gamescenes.org/2009/11/interview-tobias-bernstrup-and-palle-torsson-museum-meltdown-1996.html

[6] From the press release to the exhibition Museum Meltdown at Moderna Museet in Stockholm. Link:
http://www.palletorsson.com/mmhome/MAIN.html

[7] "Interview: Martin Berghammer's RELOAD exhibition (Shift e.V Gallery in Berlin, 1999)" by Mathias Jansson. Link:
http://www.gamescenes.org/2010/02/interview-martin-berghammer-reload-exhibition-shift-ev-gallery-in-berlin-1999-.html

"First Museum Shooters". In "First Museum Shooters" artist re-create real exhibition spaces and in this virtual interactive arena the forces of popular culture and high culture clash together in a violent and often bloody confrontation. On one side, the established art institution with its unique irreplaceable works of art, exhibited as precious relics, and on the other side the digital artwork that can be mass produced, copied and distributed via the Internet. "First Museum Shooters" can be interpreted as a metaphor for an ongoing paradigm shift in art, it is a metaphor for the struggle between the old art vs the new art. There is also a metaphor of how different generations consume culture. The older generation is more accustomed to passively consume art in institutions, stated in the expression "go and look at art", while young people today expect to be able to participate in and create their own art experience. The older generation, are in the game metaphor, the monsters who defends and preserves the institutional 'high culture" while the younger generation, the player, create their own art experience by mixing elements from high culture and popular culture and melting them together in new impressions and experiences in an interactive Game Art. Within the framework of the virtual world, the player can break all the conventions and rules surrounding the real art exhibition. He can do everything that is normally forbidden to do as loudly destroying art objects.

A Meta-Level
The Australian artists Stephen Honegger and Anthony Hunt's contribution to the genre is a bit different. There work *Container* was showed for the first time in 2002 at Gertrude Contemporary Art Space in Melbourne, Australia.[8] *Cointainer* consists of a setup where a copy of a real container is placed inside the gallery. Of course, the visitor asks himself how did they mange to get such a large shipping container into a small gallery? It can hardly have come through the door. The answer is inside the container where

---

[8] "Interview: Stephen Honegger's "Container" (2002) and "Escape from Woomera" (2003)" by Mathias Jansson. Link:
http://www.gamescenes.org/2010/06/interview-steve-.html

you can watch a video. The video is a machinima made using the computer game *Half-Life*, and shows how an unknown person breaks into the gallery by climbing in through a window at the back of the gallery. The unknown person then seeks his way through the building through corridors and staircases, until he finally arrives at the gallery. In the gallery he opens a secret hatch in the wall and presses a button. The ceiling of the gallery opens and the container is slowly lowered into the room. The unknown intruder then retrieves a gun and walks up to the container and opens the door. Inside the container there are a man looking at a video. The unknown intruder simply shoots down the man and here ends the movie, and also the explanation of how the container ended up in the gallery.

The original idea to *Container* came from a need to create a dark space in the gallery to view a video. The solution was to create a container in the gallery and also making a fictional story about how it ended up in the gallery. The visitor sits inside a proper container and sees a movie that shows how the container has come into the room and how the person in the film enters the container and shoots the viewer. It's an artwork about the creation of an artwork and therefore you could say there is a meta-level included in *Container*. In other examples of "First Museum Shooters" you will also find this kind of meta-level. As visitor you participate in different narratives levels. The artwork is showed in a physical real exhibition space in which the visitor enters, but the visitor also steps in as a viewer and player of a virtual copy of the exhibition space. To draw a parallel with the theatre, the visitor is not only a person in the audience looking at the play but he also steps up on stage and start to act and became a part of the play he is viewing. The visitor is taking part both in the physical exhibition and the virtual exhibition, he moves between different narrative levels in the artwork. In that way you can see "First Museum Shooters" as a form of meta-art, which discusses and examines the experience of art in museums and galleries.

Everything I Shoot is Art
In connection with the 2006 graduation show at the School of the Art Institute of Chicago artist Chris Reilly made a reconstructed of the entire exhibition, 4500 square feet spread over three floors, with the help of computer game *Half Life 2*. Reilly works, with the long title: *Everything I Do Is Art, But Nothing I Do Makes Any Difference, Part II: Or: How I Learned to Stop Worrying and Love the Gallery*.[9] A title that alludes to Stanley Kubrick famous film *Dr. Strangelove or: How I Learned to Stop Worrying and Love the Bomb* from 1964 with Peter Sellers in the lead role. Anyone who visited the thesis exhibition in Chicago could walk around in the real exhibition, but also make a virtual visit. In the virtual version you had to deal with some nasty monsters as in many other "First Museum Shooters". In Reilly artwork you can also shoot and destroy the artworks in the exhibition, but it is also possible to pick up paint cans around the building and shoot at them. The result is a kind of "shooting painting", where the paint can explodes and makes formation in different colours on the gallery walls. Maybe Reilly had Niki de Saint classic work of art *Shooting Paintings* in mind when he included this feature. It was between the years 1961 to 1962 as Niki de Saint Phalle did 12 performances in which she used a salon rifle to shot at paint container mounted at reliefs and sculptures. When the shot hit the container the paint spread over the object and formed a "Shooting painting". For Saint Phalle it was a statement that she as a woman could shoot her way in to the male occupied sphere of art, but it was also a new way of looking at painting. In a known quote she said:

"*Ready. Aim. Fire. Red, yellow, blue – the painting is Crying, the painting is dead. I have killed the painting. It is reborn. War with no victims.*"[10]

---

[9] http://www.chris-reilly.org/art/everything-pt2/
[10] p.285. "Theories and Documents of Contemporary Art: A Sourcebook of Artists' Writings" by Kristine Stiles and Peter Selz, (Berkeley : Univ. of California Press, 1996).

A quote that just as well could be use to describe the genre of "First Museum Shooters". Videogames can be compared to a form of new real-time paintings and when artists use the FPS games to create new art forms, they are literal shooting there way into the art history. Especially in works as Arsdoom and Museum Meltdown you can see that the artists are killing and destroying the old paintings and simultaneously creating a new form of digital paintings on the screen. After fifteen years we still see new examples of "First Museum Shooters". The Swedish artist Paul Steen has for example created *Art Assault* a modification of the free open source FPS game, *Assault Cube*.

"The computer controlled bots are named after the 100 most successful artists according to artfacts.net. In Team Deathmatch mode the bots and the player are randomly parted into two teams, Inside and Outside. The maps in the game are based on real life artist run galleries or alternative museums."[11] You can choose between 10 different maps including Magasin3, Stockholm, PS1, New York. TATE Modern, London, Westwerk, Hamburg and Worm, Rotterdam.

One more example in the genre is Michiel Van Der Zander's machinima *Pwned Paintings #2* from 2008.[12] In this machinima we see a character moving around in an art historic collection. The view is not first person, rather third person, found in games as *Max Payne*. Armed with a rifle the character moves around in the galleries shooting at the painting so they fall of the wall. Pwned is an expression used in videogames as Counterstrike, and to say "You just got pwned!" is a way to humiliate and show domination over an opponent that got soundly defeated. In the same way van Der Zanden pwned the established artworld. The statement is clear: The traditional art and art institutions have been defeated, a new

---

[11] http://www.paulsteen.se/aa.html
[12] Link: http://www.gamescenes.org/2010/01/game-art-michiel-van-de-zandens-museum-killer-2008.html

generation of artists are taking over, artists that will shoot there way into the art history and bring there own culture and expressions with them, in the same way as previous generation of artist has done before them.

The essay was first published in Hz-Journal #16.

Daniel Botz: The demoscene as Game Art's prehistory

When did artists begin to use video games as a means of expression, as a "raw material" to create art? Many regard Orhan Kipcak's ArsDoom debut at Ars Electronica in Linz as the breakthrough for a cross-media set of practices otherwise known as Game Art. Obviously, videogame-based artistic interventions did exist before ArsDoom. In fact, artists have been tinkering with the playful medium since its first appearance, in the early 1970s. However, these modifications and experiments were not "officially" recognized by the Artworld as such, that is, as forms of art. At that time, the boundaries between game players and artists were porous, undetermined. Unsurprisingly, Anne-Marie Schleiner's exhibition Cracking the Maze: Game Plug-ins and Patches as Hacker Art (1999) - one of the first milestones of Game Art history - featured not only artists but also regular players who hacked and modified games. In some cases, the outcomes were indistinguishable.

This does not come as a surprise, considering that early artistic experiments did not significantly differ from the hacks and mods created by players around the world. Thanks to the proliferation of first-person shooters (FPS), players used tools and editors to create new levels, characters, and maps that expanded the game world. Several artists used the same tools to create artistic projects that are now regarded as the first manifestations of Game Art.
This account, however, is partial, as it underplays the role played by home and microcomputers in the early 1980s. Companies such as Amstrad, Sinclair, Commodore and Atari introduced computers that became extremely popular in Europe and in the United States. Unlike game consoles, these affordable and inexpensive machines were programmable, customizable, and relatively powerful. Moreover, their popularity transcended gamers and bedroom coders. Several contemporary artists started to use these devices to make art. One of those avant-garde artists was Andy Warhol.
In an interview published on Amiga World (February 1986), Warhol discusses the impact of the Commodore Amiga on the artworld. His comments on the future of computers as artistic tools are prophetic:

- *"Do you think that computers will play a larger and larger role in art?"* The interviewer asks.
- *"Huh, yeah, I think after graffiti art, they probably will. When the machine comes out fast enough. It will probably take over from the graffiti kids."*

Andy Warhol paints Debbie Harry on an Amiga at the Commodore Amiga product launch press conference in 1985. But not even Warhol realized that the new digital graffiti generation was already active. Their playground was not the art gallery or the museum, but the online demoscene. In the recently published "Kunst, Code und Maschine. Die Ästhetik der Computer-Demoszene" (Transcript Verlag), Daniel Botz discusses the artistic implications of the demoscene. Created for the specific goal of sharing pirated copies of videogames, the demoscene quickly evolved into a kind of geographically distributed creative lab, an incubator for new digital aesthetics. Different cracking groups from all over the world – but mostly concentrated in Europe - competed against each other to break the copy protections and share the new games as quickly as possible. The crackers added a short intro, also known as cracktro, to the pirated game. This short animation displayed flashy effects meant to showcase their programming skills. These coders created "impossible" things considering the the available resources and by doing so they unleashed a bew form of competitive art practice within their community. The cracktro was, simultaneously, the artist's signature and its artwork: in this case, the map and the territory coincided. The animated intro was both a demonstration of skills(the cracker's) and power (the machine's). These early demos and animations can be regarded as the prehistory of Game Art as cracking and animation are practices of game modification with overtly aesthetic ambitions. Later on, these animations evolved into independent demos, and many of the demoscenes players became game designers.

When did the demoscene start and why?
-The first demos appeared between 1985/1986 within the European cracker scene. They were produced with the Commodore 64 home

computer. Visually, they did not differ very much from the usual intros which were linked to cracked games and usually consisted of colorful logotypes, scroll messages and simple effects like moving rasterbars. But the "stand-alone" demos always offered an extra functionality to be worth being spreaded alongside the pirated games via the mail and BBS network of the cracker scene.

This functionality could be a musical soundtrack separated from a game to be enjoyed without having to play all the levels, it could be a self-drawn picture, which always needed to come in an executable format to be displayed, or maybe an unseen effect of the computer's video hardware. Examples of the latter include removing the sideborders of the C64 screen to expand the display area, drawing scroll messages with screen-size letters or applying all kinds of wave and distortion movement to the graphical content.

Who created these demos?

- With the development of these effect-oriented programming techniques many people who used to crack games specialized in democoding. Other scene members never had a background in the illegal cracker scene, like for example the British Compunet-scene which was based on an UK-wide network service or amateur coders who used to publish their productions in computer magazines. But still in the Amiga 500 scene of the early 1990s it was common for the big cracker organisations like Red Sector Inc., Alpha Flight, Anarchy or Crystal to employ more or less independent teams of coders and artists for making demos under their group label.

And what was the purpose? Was it artistic or was it a way to show the world how skilled you were on programming and manipulate the hardware?

- The original purpose of a demo can be characterized as digital graffiti, leaving colorful footprints inside the traffic of electronic goods. It was an adolescent form of self-expression behind the handle of a "computer hacker" and at the same time a subcultural set of aesthetic practice which grounded in the cracker scene. While computer game piracy undermined the economic power of the software manufacturers, democoding questioned the computer industry's cultural dominance. In the end, both an employed game developer at a big company and a kid who bought the computer had to use the same set of machine instructions, the same color palette and the same pixel matrix of the hardware. This encouraged the teenager amateurs to challenge the media industry not only by reverse engineering their products but also by "We can do it better!".

What about the aesthetics of the demoscene? Were the demos connected to the ArtWorld at all? Where did the demoscene artists find their inspirations?
-In the beginning of the demoscene there was almost no awareness of artistic concepts nor attitudes, be it through academic studies or artistic self-reflection. Program routines, musical compositions and pixel drawings were judged by technical skills. Adapted motifs were found in popular culture, for example movie posters, record sleeves, comic drawings or paintings by fantasy illustrators. But with the decline of the illegal scene, scrolltexts and disk magazines, the communication channels of the crackers, lost their function of announcing cracks and greeting or insulting other groups.
This content was replaced by a vital discourse about artistic quality and the need for aesthetic innovation, which made clear that while there is an certain agreement upon what is called a demo, there are totally different approaches to art and design within the demoscene. Thus, scene communication serves as a way of scene-inherent art criticism, which always tries to determine the parameters for a form of design which has no purpose outside itself. Still, demo coders draw their inspirations from popular media, for example computer games, movies and music videos but the more self-reflective the demoscene got in the last ten years with sceners growing up, joining university studies and connecting in Internet forums, the more it is being discussed whether a computer demo could be a piece of art itself.

The interview took place in September 2011.

Orhan Kipcak: "ArsDoom" (1995)

ArsDoom is widely regarded as one of the first examples of artistic modifications of videogames. Created in 1995 by Orhan Kipcak and Reini Urban, ArsDoom was shown at the Ars Electronica Festival in Linz the same year. Using the Doom II engine and Autodesk' AutoCAD software, Kipcak and Urban created a virtual copy of the Brucknerhaus' exhibition hall and invited artists to create or submit virtual artworks that could be displayed in the new map. Armed with a shooting cross, a chainsaw or a brush the player could kill the artists and destroy all the artworks on display. Among its many merits, ArsDoom is remembered for redefining the very notion and role of the visitor: the user could become curator and critic as well, deciding which artists were to stay and which were to be destroyed, what to keep and what to erase for public display.

Can you tell me something about the development of ArsDoom? How and why did you decide to modify id Software's first-person shooter?

- My approach to ArsDoom was somehow framed/influenced by my background as an architect, as well as my work as an interaction designer and computer artist. In the early '90's, I began working on a series of research projects focusing on the virtualization of the exhibit experience. Back then, museums and galleries were interested in using the web in innovative ways. Around that time, I also also worked on various projects for the Styrian Autumn Festival and the Venice Biennale. I created physical art for the Biennale but there was also a spin-off for the web. Back then I used VRML to create 3D simulations. VRML worked quite well but it had some limitations. And then Id Software opened up the Doom engine, allowing everybody to tinker with the Level Editor. It was such a powerful tool! It was an epiphany: I decided that I would use that technology for my next project and did not go back to VRML.

When Ars Electronica invited me to produce an artwork for the 1995 festival, I proposed and subsequently developed ArsDoom, a project that extended a virtual exhibition into the space of a computer game. This hybrid of virtual exhibition and first-person shooter was accepted and funded by Peter Weibel, the festival director.

The concept, the interaction design, the character design and its assets were created in my studio with a staff of eight assistants. Game artists and sound designers worked on the project as well, including Curd Duca, who went on to become a recognized artist in the ambient music scene. All the modules were then assembled technically by Reini Urban. Reini also programmed a little extension that bypassed the limitations of the Doom Level Editor: the original editor could only design squared rooms. But we needed a room with pointed angles in order to reproduce the complex geometry of the physical design of the Ars Electronica center, the Brucknerhaus.

For the virtual exhibition, I invited several artists to produce virtual art pieces which could be displayed within the game level. Furthermore I let my students of the University of Applied Arts in Vienna design a whole room in the virtual Brucknerhaus. Every artist was told that their art pieces would be shown only to be destroyed. I'm happy to report that all of them agreed.

What made you decide to use game-based technology to create an artwork?

-Three reasons: First: I think that using a technology in ways that the designer/producer did not plan or expect is a very interesting and innovative strategy – using a first-person shooter to create an art exhibition allowed us to broaden the cultural spectrum, to subvert some of the expectations associated with an art event/experience and to introduce new formats. Additionally, i was fascinated by the metaphorical power of computer games in general and first-person shooters in particular. The idea of using this medium was very appealing to me. There are obvious similarities between a battlefield and the Artworld. The competitiveness of the artscene reflects the darwinian nature of videogame landscapes - in a sense, the videogame made the invisible conflicts of the artworld "real", explicit and visible, albeit in a playful way.

Also games were - and still are today - a vital part of our culture. Their aesthetics is the aesthetics of our culture. Using a game engine as a creative tool was for me also a polemic and offensive statement, a design choice meant to attack, frontally, the computer art scene. Last but not least: I chose a videogame for technical and practical reasons. The Doom Engine was an open-source solution, easy to handle and very popular at the time. It made our life so much easier!

What's your own relationships to videogames?
-I've always seen them as an important catalyst for new developments in the field of human – computer interaction. Computer games are the true avant-garde of many cultural and technical innovations. Moreover, as an interaction designer I consider computer games as a very attractive design material.

Did you play a lot of games back then? Were you a "gamer"?
-Yes, but my interest was mostly professional.

How did the public and the media react to ArsDoom?
-The reactions were extreme in both ways, good and bad. The project was harshly attacked by Linz' media as well as by some art publications. Interestingly, their arguments were very similar: ArsDoom was equated to Doom and condemned as a "fascist orgy of violence". The fact that Doom's predecessor, Wolfenstein, also created by id Software, had a rating of 16+ and older was often mentioned.
I remember a furious very personal attack: An art magazine had the headline "Orhan Kipcak – Dumm wie Doom" (literally, "Orhan Kipcak- stupid like Doom'). I was very pleased with the opponents of the project: narrow-minded dogmatists and moralists without any sense of humor. On the other hand there were very positive mentions; The BBC, RAI, ORF, Der Spiegel, numerous magazines and journals covered it in a more positive light. They seemed to appreciate and grasp the burlesque and anarchistic aspects. They also "got" and appreciated the subversive-affirmative element. Overall, the positive reactions overcome the negative. The same can be said for the visitors' feedback. ArsDoom was shown on several workstations.

It looks like you had a lot of fun creating ArsDoom?
-That's correct. My approach was certainly anarchic. I developed this project with the intention of making a point about the artscene, using a game to deliver the message. I had taught in art schools and therefore I was familiar with the rituals, the conflicts and do's and don'ts. I saw ArsDoom as an inside joke, a tongue-in-cheek take on the Artworld.

In the game you can pick up objects as Herman Nitsch's blood, Arnulf Rainer's pencils and you could flip the artworks in a George Baselitz style. What is your relationship to these artists, and why did you choose them?
-Nitsch, Rainer and Baselitz didn't provide any artworks, only the weapons that you can use in exhibition to destroy the artworks. I chose those artists because they were well known and their art had a brutal aspect to it. This is important for an ego shooter: With Arnulf Rainer you paint over artworks, with Nitsch you soak them in blood, with Baselitz you turn them upside-down. Those are significant interaction facilities for the gamer – the gameplay becomes more appealing.

When you created ArsDoom did you think you were doing something completely new fort the art world?
-I knew that at that time no one had thought about using game engines as an art tool. But I wasn't surprised that in the following year other projects like this popped up almost everywhere. As Adorno wrote: "The art needs to evolve in order to reach the level of the technology of its times". And games are a medium that has defined the state of the art of digital design for more than twenty years. Anyway, in the field of media art it's some kind of a natural law that the gadgets used by teenagers today will become festival-material tomorrow.
By the way: that year (1995) I develop a series of projects with my students in Graz which used Doom as space-simulator. The Doom Level editor was a great tool and not using it for other projects felt like a missed opportunity.

Last but not least: are there any easter eggs in ArsDoom?
-There's a room in ArsDoom in which a misshapen "monster" (A futile attempt by Reini Urban to design a monster) is hidden. If I remember correctly you can get to it by passing the gallery.

Some closing comments about the follow up ArsDoom2:
-A decade after ArsDoom I told Peter Weibel, back then head of the Ars Electronica and fiunder of ArsDoom, that I would have loved to create a new version. I persuaded him with the argument that, with the original ArsDoom, we'd created a new art genre, a genre that was still fresh and popular ten years after its debut. Weibel, who is by now head of the ZKM (Zentrum für Kunst und Medien) in Karlsruhe, accepted and funded the project: we followed the same formula that we developed for ArsDoom from 1995 (virtual exhibition/kill the artist/destroy the artworks) and the same artists were involved, but this time we modeled the ZKM and used state-of-the-art authoring software. I finished this project in 2004 using Virtools. The technical implementation was made by Immersive Systems in Stuttgart, Germany. After solving a series of technical problems with Immersive the Virtools-job was finally well completed in Leipzig by Günter Baumgart, a very good software engineer. The updated interaction, character and environmental design were produced by my studio in Graz, Austria.

The interview took place in November 2009.

Tobias Bernstrup and Palle Torsson: "Museum Meltdown" (1996)

In 1996, two Swedish art students created what is now considered the first example of an artistic modification of a videogame in Scandinavia, if not in the world. Palle Torsson and Tobias Bernstrup started their artistic career with a scandal and continued to push the boundaries of art with "Museum Meltdown", a piece where the relatively conservative conventions of the art world imploded when they collided with videogames. "Museum Meltdown" was shown at the biennale "Borealis 8" at Arken Museum of Contemporary Art outside Copenhagen in Denmark. It generated a stir within the artworld and was soon imitated. The exhibit catalogue of "Borealis 8: The Scream", lists such artists as Vanessa Beecroft, Peter Land, Olafur Eliasson and Tony Oursler. Then your eyes encounter the names of two art students from Sweden who just created a hyper-violent videogame titled "Museum Meltdown".

How did you mange to get invited to "Borealis 8: The Scream" with a videogame?
-After causing some minor scandal and debate with a censored internet piece in 1995 titled "Joined Hands", curator Kim Levin became familiar with our work. After receiving an official invitation to join the show, we suggested a radical idea: creating a computer game based on the Arken Museum, which was hosting the event.

Were you at this time aware that other artists also were working with videogames? For example Orhan Kipcak brought ArsDoom to Ars Electronica 1995?
-Our main source of inspiration was the game Doom. We learned about ArsDoom some years later. Even if these two projects share a similar logic, they are also significantly different; ArsDoom focuses on the concept of the artist and the conventions of artistic practice by replacing the weapon with a paint brush. For our project, on the other hand, it was important not to alter the narrative of the game

and its arsenal in order to polarize both the game world and the artworld.

"Museum Meltdown" was created by hacking Duke Nukem 3D. Why did you choose this game instead of Doom?
-Duke Nukem 3D was the first game bundled with a level editor called 'Build' and it had a more advanced graphic engine, that gave us more possibilities to recreate the somewhat complex architecture of the museum.

How did you work together to create "Museum Meldown"?
-We had some earlier experience in writing games for the old Commodore machines back in the 1980s, but none of us had ever modified a 3D game up to that point. It took us one month of playing and researching and one month to design the level. We were working in shifts, the level editor was running 24/7...

Is it true that it was a guest teacher who introduced you to the art of modding?
-Correct. That was the animator and artist Richard Wright who was a guest teacher at the Royal College University of Fine Arts in Stockholm. We started discussing Doom after he had seen us playing it day and night...

You made two sequels. Can you tell something about the reactions from the public, critics and curators?
-The curator Kestutis Kuizinas at The Contemporary Art Center in Vilnius got really excited and invited us to do a new project for the exhibition "Funny vs Bizarre" in 1997 at the art center. In 1999 David Elliott who was the director at Moderna Museet also liked our project and wanted us to do a version in Stockholm. Then later the French curator Laurance Dreyfus invited us to the Lyon Biennale in 2001. But it took quite some time before the actual discussion on the potential of video games as an artistic medium actually began. I can think of an article published in late 2001 by The New York Times and an exhibition that took place at the San Fransisco MoMA in the same year... These two events kind of marked out the path.

After that, other writers, curators and critics slowly started to notice the phenomenon.

"Museum Meltdown" is a landmark in the history of interactive art. But did any art museum or art gallery purchase it?
-Good question, our dealer at that time have suggested the Moderna Museet to buy the fantastic piece twice, but they deemed it as too expensive... Or maybe they have not understood the unique quality of this piece. Its aura, if you will...

Finally, are there any Easter eggs in the game?
-Would have been a really nice idea. There are some hidden rooms with surprises though.

The interview took place in November 2009.

Antonio Riello: "Italiani Brava Gente" (1996)

Nowadays, several artists use videogames for purposes that include political and artistic expression. Examples that come to mind are Gonzalo Frasca's celebrated September 12th, a Flash-game about terrorism in the world post-911 or Escape from Woomera, a modification of Half-Life, about a refugee camp in Woomera, Australia. The common denominator of all these interactive artworks is that the artists involved wanted to make a point about a current issue or event. Serious games or political games, however, are nothing new. In 1996, Italian artist Antonio Riello - who calls himself "an ideas tamer. One of those who normally feed themselves in the contemporary art pasture" - designed a game titled Italiani Brava Gente (literally, Italians Good People) about "illegal" (i.e. unregulated) immigration. In the game, Albanians immigrants are trying to reach Italian shores by boat and the player must prevent them to achieve such goal.

The title "Italiani Brava Gente" has different layers of meaning. Can you elaborate?
-Literally, it means "Italians [are] Good People". It is a cliché often used by the most populist Italian media to claim that Italians are "better" than other when it comes to kindness, humanity, and openness toward other cultures. In this case, the title is meant to be ironic. There is often a huge gap between clichés and reality. Occasionally, that gap becomes visible. Fiction becomes friction. And trouble ensues...

What the cultural background of your videogame?
-In the early Nineties, Italy faced waves of illegal immigrations from the Balkan regions, especially from Albania. For those who don't know, Albania used to be an Italian "protectorate" during the brief but intense Fascist "Empire". Italy, however, was not prepared to handle this issue. Illegal immigration proved to be problematic on several levels – political, social and cultural. Above all, it created all sorts of problems: the paradox is that Italians have emigrated all

over the world for at least a century, and now they seemed unable to manage immigration in their own country. The problem persists today. It is actually becoming more and more of an issue.

Why did you choose to make a videogame about illegal immigration?
-I felt responsible, as an artist, to address this situation by creating an artwork that could portray a complex situation and I found that the game medium could provide that kind of complexity. At the same time, games are intuitive enough to be understood by many, unlike most contemporary art, which is cryptic and elitist. I thought that this format was more appropriate to express the tragi-comic national embarrassment and discomfort generated by modern day immigration. Those feelings, by the way, were a manifestation of Belpaese's inner xenophobia and racism. Moreover, I was fascinated by digital games' many paradoxes: virtual environments are spaces where Western cultures can enact their fantasies of domination, violence, neo-imperialism, and prevarication. It is as if we erased our deepest urges and desires and confined them in videogames. They operate as one culture's subconscious: anything that has been prohibited in "real life" is perfectly normal and acceptable in games. Political correctness is not a rule of videogames, just an option. Thus, the video game was the ideal choice for my project. And I chose the simplest format possible: an old school shoot'em up, which was subsequently mixed with Italian "huffy-duffy" national folklore and politics: the official rhetorical language of politicians, the National Anthem, "O Sole Mio" songs, and idiotic, pedantic visuals, which evoked the iconography used in Italian primary schools. I wanted to give the game the appearance of government propaganda. The goal of "Italiani Brava Gente" is extremely simple. After selecting the difficulty level, the player has to control a turret located on the South East coast and sink all the approaching ships. The idea is that immigrants from Albania are "space invaders" who are threatening the Belpaese's lifestyle and values, therefore they deserve to be annihilated. However, in the end the player cannot keep up and loses. It's just a matter of time before hordes of immigrants overcome the defender.

How did you design the game? Did you use other interactive artworks as models for your project?
-I designed the concept, script and the visuals. An Italian coder working for a game design company helped me with the programming. He used Macromedia Flash to put all the pieces together. The company he was working for, by the way, no longer exists. As I mentioned before, I did not explicitly use any existing games as a "model", but I tried to emulate the game mechanics of seminal titles such as Space Invaders. I felt that Taito's arcade was a fitting metaphor for Italy in the early and mid Nineties.

When you released the game, the reaction from the press was controversial, to say the least. Why?
-Two reasons. First, the Italian media was outraged that somebody would use a game to make a point about a sensitive social issue. Games were – and still are, in many ways – discriminated and ostracized by the so-called intellectuals. Behind its hip facade, Italian culture is old, reactionary and conservative. Second, the media saw me as a bogeyman. When the game was released – between 1996 and 1997 – the press called it a "social nightmare created by a monstrous mind" (that would be me). Italians don't like to be reminded that they can be racist too. They are too enamored with the "postcard view" created by Hollywood movies and supported by local advertising and marketing. We need to maintain the fantasy for the sake of tourism, which is one of the few healthy industries that we have. There is an unwritten rule that says that you cannot mess with the fairy-tale ideology of Italianism. The most important newspapers and TV channels called Italiani Brava Gente a "politically-incorrect game for right wing hooligans", "trash", "juvenile provocation". Interestingly, in 2009, the Northern League party – [a political group that advocates the separation of Northern Italy from the South, currently an ally of Berlusconi's right wing government Ed.] – released an openly racist videogame that used the same mechanics seen in Italiani Brava Gente. I am happy to report that, once again, Contemporary Art can be prophetic, although reality is always one step ahead.

Where was the game exhibited?
-It was presented in some solo shows (Torch Gallery Amsterdam, I'll Ponte Gallery Roma, Artra Gallery Milano and others). It has also been shown at Meran Kunstverein, Placentia Gallery, Wolfsburg Art Museum, and recently at at South Pacific University Art Gallery in California. Albanian artist Gentian Shkurti produced another videogame, GO WEST, that somehow mirrored mine: here too Albanians try to reach the Italian shores. We presented our two games together in a unique installation at Tirana Biennale in 2001 and afterward in several other shows. In short, Italiani Brava Gente has been around quite a bit.

In 1996, could you predict the rise of serious games? Did you see their potential in influencing the contemporary art scene?
-The short answer is yes. I regard videogames' influence on the contemporary art scene as impressive. To me, games represent an autonomous medium, a medium that followed the tradition of other forms of expression. Take opera, which was originally considered lo-bro entertainment, a format which mixes Art and trashy popular culture in innovative ways. It slowly evolved only to be appropriated by the upper-class and today opera has become a niche activity used mostly as a sign of distinction – in Bourdieau's terms – for the aristocracy and for the nouveau riches. Games could follow the same path. I wanted to add, however, that term "digital" does not connotate "good, trendy contemporary art". Just because something is interactive or digital, it does not mean it possesses "quality". Clever ideas are medium-agnostic. There is nothing intrinsically artistic about games: it's how you use them that really matters. Alas, this view is not shared by many contemporary artists, who just jumped on the bandwagon. For them, videogame aesthetics are synonymous of "interesting", "smart", "brilliant". Moreover, videogames do not age well. Their planned obsolescence makes them very sensitive to aging. Thus, using a videogame for artistic purposes is very risky and potentially counter-productive, in the long run.

The interview took place in November 2009.

Konrad Becker: "Synreal: The Unreal Modification" (1998)

In 1998, Austrian collective Netbase t0 organized an exhibition about the potential of the emerging hyperspace called "Synworld". "Synreal: The Unreal Modification" was part of the main exhibition, and it is now remembered as one of the first collective shows where artists were invited to create Game Art-based installations, in this case Unreal (1998) by Epic Games. The artist line-up featured, among the others, Axel Stockburger, Basicray, Dextro, fuchs-eckermann, Glow, jodi.org, Margarete Jahrmann, Kandyman, Max Moswitzer, Robert Adrian X, August Black, Markus Seidl, Synreal t0 and Vuk Cosic. That exhibition was curated by Konrad Becker, a hypermedia researcher and interdisciplinary content developer, director of the Institute for New Culture Technologies/t0 and initiator of Public Netbase and World-Information.org. Since 1979 he has been active in electronic media as an artist, writer, composer, curator, producer and organizer of numerous intermedia productions, exhibitions, and event designs for international festivals and cultural institutions.

What were Netbase t0's goals?
-Netbase started out in 1994 as the first internet venue for artists in Austria as well as a platform that provided services to cultural workers, mediation, debate, and lobbying for media culture. (Public) Netbase was forced to shut down after many years of intense political struggles...

What was "Synreal"?
-Synreal was a part of "Synworld," an exhibition and conference, about the interrelations of play, work, and hyperspace. Synworld was not just about gaming, even though electronic entertainment played a major role in the show, and there were other games and 3D spaces not based on the Unreal. Going from a "flat" 2D image to 3D significantly augments the information space. For visualization and information architecture, which functions with large data sets

and dynamic complexity, the expansion of Euclidean space into the field of hyper-dimensionality, even more than 3 dimensions, has become a necessity.

How did you select the artists to the exhibition? There were not many Game Artists back then.
-I choose some of the artists that were using games as a means of expression and that I thought might be interested in the project. It is true, there were very few artists working with games or even 3D games back then. As a matter of fact, we specifically commissioned them pieces or projects. We also persuaded some of them that games were artistically interesting... Not all the artists recognized the potential of gaming. Some, however, are tinkering with games even today.

"Synreal" features a series of artistic interventions based on the Unreal engine. Why did you choose this particular game?
-Well, I have been experimenting with the rather unreliable Quake engine/editor before, only to discover that it was very, very tedious for more complex levels. We had so many crashes which obliterated hours and days of work. Unreal provided a much better design experience. It was better on every level. Plus, it was free. I first build a level and then we offered support to all the artists that might need assistance.

Was there a discussion at this time about how videogames could be used by artists in the future?
There was no doubt that gaming was bound to become "the future" of artistic experimentation. This is why I pushed the artists since day one. Multidimensional visualization and engineering was one of the key topics of the conference.

But there must been others around you thinking that videogames were nothing more than entertainment, something for kids, right?
-Oh, yeah. And they still do think they are nothing more than a pastime, a trivial pursuit, sometime to entertain kids.

What is your own experience with videogames?
-My first videogame experiences can be traced back to the Commodore 64. I have been exploring all the different kinds of electronic arts, from music to first digital video/animation. At that time, I was still very much following what games are out and what options the could open up. For me, to start with, it was very exciting to create "live" 3D "video". Originally, I created VRML files which could be used as a "walk-trough" as part of my settings and performances. Think, for instance, of "Next5Minute", 1996, which was shown at Paradiso Amsterdam.

Would you say, in the Nineties, artists used videogames mainly because they offered a cheap and easy way to create and navigate 3D spaces, unlike more expensive, dedicated 3D applications?

Well, that was definitely one of the appeals of using games! Even if you had accesso to expensive 3D software that wouldn't help you much in creating complex "_live_ 3D" and at that time, huge workstations like SGI machines were already on the way out. Second, editors for narrative gameplay and AI programming are necessary. I personallydeveloped a computer game for a SGI machine which debuted at a festival in Iin 1994, called Brain Vader, a "brainwave-controlled virtual environment, musical shoot'em up and man-machine adventure" but not a mod.

Finally, do you think that artist and game designer today are using the full potential in videogames?
-Gaming today is huge industry, akin to the film business. The standards and quality trademarks have become very high. At the same time, it feels that the genres have become quite narrowly defined and there is much less experimentation. At the same time, independent projects are starting to appear here and there. There is definitely more funding available in the so-called art-house cinema than in Game Art, mostly because we rely on archaic nature of what constitutes "art" and "culture". But it will change.

The interview took place in November 2009.

Anne-Marie Schleiner: "Cracking the Maze" (1999)

In July 1999, artist and scholar Anne-Marie Schleiner curated the exhibition "Cracking the Maze: Game Plug-ins and Patches as Hacker Art" at San Jose State University in San Jose, California. The exhibition featured both artists and game hackers and presented artistic modifications of commercial videogames.

How did "Cracking the Maze" come to be?
- Back in the mid-1990's my thesis in Computers in Fine Art, at CADRE program at San Jose State University in California, was a game modification and sculptural interactive installation based on the modification called Madame Polly (Polly from Polygon--the planes that 3-D game space is built from.) In the process of making this mod I encountered the world of game hackers, skinners, patchers, wadders and whatever else people who would make alterations in games in micro and macro ways were called. They shared their mods online and also shared the software tools and techniques that they used to make them. So my first contact was technical but when I discovered the underworld of modification, which seemed much more experimental in many ways (culturally, gender-wise, thematically, and potentially ludically) than the original commercial games they modified, it occurred to me it would be interesting to invite artists to get their hands on these tools and to make modifications with them.

How did you select the artists for "Cracking the Maze"? There couldn't have been too many artists experimenting with videogames at that time, right?
- I circulated an online call for entries describing the curatorial concept of "Cracking the Maze" and over the course of 9 months artists responded. For instance net art duo JoDi were already working on modifiying Wolfenstein, 3-D. Jason Huddy's Los Disneys was already completed and I contacted him directly to ask for his participation, and some of the other artists who responded to my call were in the midst of creating pieces. For other interested artists like Josephine Starrs and Leon Cmeleiwski I helped procure free

games and modification software and games, writing to a couple game companies like ID software to see if they would be interested in sponsoring the show in some capacity. Bungie, makers of Mac game Marathon (later fated to be bought by Microsoft and to make Halo), offered free copies of their games and modification software to the "Cracking the Maze" artists, which luckily was the same game I had modified to create Madame Polly so I was also offering the artists some technical advice. Feeling like there was still a lack of mods intervening in more aggressively artistic and aesthetic ways, I snuck a new mod of my own into "Cracking the Maze" called Epilepsy Virus Patch under an artist persona of mine Parangari Cutiri (in those days, before social software tied down our identities, it was common for digital artists to have anonymous extra artist personas). So I was technical support, curator and an artist for "Cracking the Maze", a mix maybe as unholy as the relationship between the commercial PC game industry and the gift ecology of game modding.

The exhibition also featured a series of game hackers. Did you see any difference between them and the artists in the exhibition?
- Of course there are differences but in "Cracking the Maze" it seemed strategic to blur those differences. I think many online creators, whether they are posting remakes of Youtube videos or customized game avatar skins, do not consider themselves artists and they do not have artistic training. They remain innocent (maybe happily) of previous artistic tactics which foreshadow their creative processes, such as the collaborative cafe games of the Surrealists or Marcel Duchamp's found objects. These processes, which I am calling "ludic mutation" in my current Phd research, are about changing the given, metamorphosis, cultural hacking that has the potential to travel along contagious vectors, especially in the online medium of culture. Fine artists' game modifications, on the other hand, I often wish were more contagious than they have been so far. The game industry has yet to adopt a more fragmented, less mimetic experimental approach to virtual 3-D space, with few mostly Japanese exceptions like the PlayStation music game Rez or Katamari Damacy. In fact one encounters the opinion that good art

cannot be a good game. This reveals assumptions about what constitutes good game play, however play is not necessarily rule bound but also chaotic (paidia), destructive and creative. Generes such as sandbox games indicate a broadened approach to play appearing even in the industry..well I can go on and on about theories of play etc from my current writing for my dissertation and from my classes teaching game design at the National University of Singapore so I will stop here.

In your curator's note, you wrote: "Many artists, art critics, new media critics and theoreticians have expressed a disdain for games and game style interactivity, in fact, to describe an interactive computer art piece as "too game-like" is a common pejorative." So how did the public, critics, and the visitor react to the exhibition?
-If imitation is flattery yes there were some exhibits that borrowed a very similar line-up of artists as "Cracking the Maze", which was originally created outside the umbrella of any art intuition or festival as a purely online art show. Terms such as "patching" which appeared in my curatorial statement and that were actually not common vernacular in the game mod community were key indicators of unrefer nced influence in the descriptions of other shows :). There was a response from the press, some mention in articles in the art section of the New York Times. American museums never did seem to keen on the idea of games as art but some European digital art festivals were interested, for example I got an invitation to curate a small online show for the Sonar digital music festival in Barcelona which I called Snow Blossom House and I managed to bring a couple of the same artists with this show, although Snow Blossom House was not exclusively focused on games.

"Cracking the Maze" was an online exhibition, why didn't you make a real exhibition in an exhibition hall with computers?
-Anne-Marie Schleiner: I thought more people would have exposure through the Internet than if the mods were installed in a local gallery in one location, even if online one only could experience the small animated gifs(Internet pages have grown in resolution size

since then), game mod screenshots and descriptions. At the time this was also a conscious political decision to privilege the Internet as a medium over what I saw as more limited elitist art world venues.

At that time, did you believe that videogames could become a new important medium for artistic expressions? Could you foresee that digital games were bound to become one of the most popular forms of entertainment and an academic discipline?
-Of course I envisioned games as important medium for artmaking, thus my efforts to get game software modification tools into the hands of other artists besides myself for "Cracking the Maze". And yes even back then in the late 1990's I was interested in games as a subject of serious academic research. I submitted the short rationale I wrote for my Madame Polly game patch creation to the journal Leonardo who published it later as a revised article called "Does Lara Croft wear fake polygons" in 1999. I have always been critically fascinated with games but I could not foresee how the field of ludology would take off, and in many ways I am critical of a thread of reductionism structuralism within ludology that forecloses artistic intervention and creativity in relation to play -this is another area I have found it necessary to entangle with in my current research.

"Cracking the Maze" is still available on the net, but for how long? Games and technology are changing so fast... Will it be possible to preserve the history of the early Game Art for the generations to come?
- Yes, I am grateful to my alma matter, CADRE and their online graduate student journal Switch for continuing to host "Cracking the Maze". The ephemerality of digital art is a big problem that has not been adequately solved, and maybe this also has something to do with its charm. I leave this question to more capable people like Jon Ippolito or gallerists of digital media art to resolve these issues... I have sold a few collectable betacam SP videos and screenshot prints of my own software art to collectors but how long does video really last and is this really an adequate representation of interactive

works? It takes a lot of effort to look at my own work from older platforms even. It would be nice if people in the cultural industry could do something about the longevity of artworks in this variable medium.

The interview took place in December 2009.

Martin Berghammer: "RELOAD" (1995)

Martin Berghammer is a visual artist, programmer and director and co-curator of Shift e.V. in Berlin. In 1995 he curated the exhibition "RELOAD" at Shift e.V Gallery where four artists designed special levels for the videogame Quake.

Can you tell me something about the creation of Shift e.V gallery in 1995?
- Shift e.V. was a privately held non-profit art-organization founded in 1995 by myself and a group of Berlin-based artists. We provided a platform for exhibitions, lectures, and events that dealt with crossover-tendencies in contemporary art. After six years and nearly twenty-five exhibitions Shift closed its doors in spring 2001.

What's your relationship to art and videogames?
-I am an artist, I started as a painter in the 1980s, later switched to installation, and worked with different media including Super-8 film and video. I founded Shift in 1995 and ran it as a director and curator for six years. I became interested in video games in the early nineties, I played some "harmless" adventure-games (like Myst). At that time I discovered DVD-projects from artists and musicians that were built around a game aspect, such as "Freak Show" from the band "The Residents". The game Quake caught my attention not because of its furious action, but for the fact that it was the first game to allow networked (IP-based) gaming; it seemed like a good example for a 3D-environment providing real-time-interaction and - communication (chat). After becoming a gamer myself - which I felt was a necessary step in order to be able to work with it - I became aware of the various peculiar and creative aspects to the culture of gaming. Any modification of the game, of its levels and characters, required a lot of coding experiments with buggy editors and handcrafted tools released by other gamers, everything was "learning by doing". I noticed an interesting momentum here: a growing sub-culture connected to a technical revolution had begun to enter the mainstream. Such a wave could serve as a metaphor

for how culture mutates in general as well as how cultural borders are transgressed.

I found this comment about Reload very interesting: "Despite their enormous economic and social relevance, online games are still reduced to being a waste of time and appropriate only in the realm of nerds and slackers." It seems to me that the idea that videogames could be indeed art must have been regarded with disbelief and scorn at that time. On the other hand the exhibition Reload toured Germany during 1999-2001, so there must have been a growing interest in this new form of art?
-In the early nineties gaming was still an underground phenomenon, unnoticed by the mainstream, and not taken seriously in the contemporary art world. Only a few media artists worked with modifying computer code, HTML-pages and games, and formed an outsider group within the art world. Working in that field required quite a lot of technical skills, and the audience also needed a certain amount of expertise in order to fully understand the work. By the mid-nineties the aesthetics of computer-, game- and web-interfaces slowly started to invade mainstream media like news-TV, advertising or MTV-music-clips and artists became more aware of the potential of the web and virtual space as a source of material and inspiration. Through researching the topic on the web I discovered the work of some of the other artists (mentioned earlier in this interview serie) that had worked in the 3D-game space, but processing that whole phenomenon intellectually had not yet begun.

How did you select the artists for the exhibition?
-When I started to play Quake myself I immediately knew that there was an art-project somewhere in there, but didn't quite know how to approach it. In 1998, while playing online I met Florian Muser & Imre Oswald who had built a Quake-level representing the Hamburger Kunsthalle. That was a starting point; I invited them and several other artists, whose work dealt with architecture, 3D and/or internet-based media-art, to contribute to a gaming-project. Only some of them had experience with gaming and/or Quake. A bunch

of blinking computer screens in an empty room always looks a bit odd - I therefore decided to go for a "real space vs. hyperspace" concept for the show, since I thought it was important to base it within actual, physical space. The main conceptual decision we made in modifying Quake was not to deconstruct - i.e. destroy - the game but to work within the given environment and let the software be "playable" (to keep it fun...). The group working on the digital pieces quickly became a team, helping each other with the many technical challenges they were facing. Muser & Oswald's "Hamburger Kunsthalle" level was basically finished when I invited them - the piece was then later acquired by the museum. The other Quake-levels were commissioned for the show, production time was several months. We had a public Quake-server running during the exhibition that allowed players from outside to join in (you had to download and install the modified levels from our website).

The exhibition designer was Stefan Wieland. Can you explain the big idea behind his innovative and original design?
-Stefan Wieland's piece was a hybrid between sculpture and exhibition architecture, spread across all rooms, and consisted of six giant letters forming the word RELOAD. As often in his work he used a word/text-fragment as a starting point, reducing it to a simple object that still subtly referred to its original meaning. Working directly with the proportions of the exhibition space he transformed it into a sort of real world game level, playfully forcing the visitor to navigate through the gallery by climbing over and around the sculptural components. Furthermore, the sculpture, while elegantly hiding the computer hardware, served as a stand for the four terminals running the Quake-mods, as well as providing a pedestal for Astrid Herrmann's architectural models of game-space interiors. In the second edition of RELOAD that travelled to Geneva, Nuernberg, Munich, and Frankfurt we tried as a group to merge the two realms a little more, and, using the new version of the game Quake 3, we designed a virtual representation of Stefan Wieland's new sculpture as a single game-level in the form of the word LOST.

What was the reaction of the public to the exhibition?
-Well, as is often the case when people encounter a screen in an exhibition, here they were also initially in more of an observation mode. Then they would hesitatingly grab the mouse and begin to click it. Others would ask me what to do etc., so I would give them a brief introduction and show them how to get around....and off they went on a virtual stroll. The visitors familiar with games immediately felt comfortable, as well as some Turkish teenagers who came to play every afternoon with their McDonald's food in hand, as if the gallery was a gaming arcade (after a few weeks we had to kick them out though...). Once a curator stormed in and loudly declared himself to be a pacifist - later that night he was the last person to leave and we had to pull the plug on him.

What surprised you most?
-I was definitely surprised by how quickly and seriously the whole topic of games and virtual space was taken over by academia and theorists. I am stunned (and at times dismayed...) by the momentum of this technical (r)evolution, in particular by the extent to which it now overstimulates and governs our lives. The boundaries between reality and virtual space are blurred more and more: head-up-displays in cars, air-tags for cell phones, military equipment etc. You might even say that we're already living in a gamer's science-fiction world today.

The interview took place in January 2010.

Tilman Baumgärtel: "Computergames by Artist" (2003)

Tilman Baumgärtel was curator for the exhibition "Computergames by Artist" at Hartware Medien Kunst Verein, Dortmund-Hörde, (2003), which featured an amazing line-up of artists from all over the world working with videogames as Julien Alma/Laurent Hart, Cory Arcangel, Mister Ministeck Norbert Bayer, Tom Betts, Pash Buzari, Leon Cmielewski/Josephine Starrs, Arcangel Constantini, Vuk Cosic, Aurélien Froment, fuchs-eckermann, Beate Geissler/Oliver Sann, Margarete Jahrmann/Max Moswitzer, Jodi, Joan Leandre etc.

"Computergames by artist" was a large exhibition featuring 30 artists. Quite impressive! I supposed that there must have been a lot of interest in Game Art, both in terms of audience and funding, correct?
- Not really. We got some funding from the Bundeskulturstiftung, back then a very new government foundation that sponsors all kind of art activities. I think we were among the very first to apply, as they just started out then. Maybe we were lucky that not so many applied at that time. This foundation has sponsored other media and digital art activities later on, but it was never particularly high on their agenda. We also got funding from a social foundation, called Fond Soziokultur. That is probably telling, as they are mostly into social projects, not in the arts. We got an award from them as their best project in that year, though, maybe because it was so different from what they usually support. However, we also got a honorary mention from the Art Critic Organisation AICA, so it wasn't that the show was not taken seriously by art people.

In 1999, Shift e.V gallery in Berlin organized one of the first the exhibitions on Game Art in Germany. Could you describe the "climate" for Game Art in Germany in the beginning of 2000, so to speak?
- There wasn't really any "climate" for Game Art at that time. The shift people were the kind of people who are these absolute

pioneers whose contribution never gets properly acknowledged. I saw their show "Reload", and it was really what got me interested in artists working with computer games. It wasn't a genre back than, it was really just an interesting exhibition concept, and you really have to give it to them, that they commissioned original works, even though they were neither a commercial gallery nor a publicly funded art space. In fact, I wonder how they financed their activities. I have lost touch with them since, and I really regret that they are not around anymore, as they were among the few institutions that looked both at media art and regular art scene art. I guess they were really representative of that time in Berlin, where idealistic people left and right opened spaces like that. It would be much harder to do today, as even in Berlin rents went up and you cant just have an art space like that in such a central location (right on Friedrichstrasse!).

If my memory serves me right, the exhibition "Transmediale" in 2001 focussed on software art, and that was how people understood these game art works: as the next development in digital art after net art and software art. I am not sure anymore if I saw Game Art as a genre in its own right back then, probably not, as the subtitle of the show was "Computer Games by Artists", not "A presentation/retrospective of Game Art" or anything like that. I think that these kinds of labels are unproductive anyway, as the case of Game Art shows: Once you have a label like that, it turns into this little subculture, that is more interested in itself than reaching out beyond its own confines.

Anyway, the "Transmediale" on software art was what got the hArtware people interested in my project, as they had shown a presentation of software art works previously that was curated by Andreas Broeckmann, then the head of Transmediale, and his show to some extent was based on the works from that Transmediale (that might have been his first, but I am not sure, and the Transmediale website has elimanted the archive of these older shows). It had generated quite an interest in this phenomenon, and therefore it made sense to have a show on Software Art. Then Andreas hooked me up with Iris Dressler and Hans Dieter Christ, who had founded hArtware, and were still running it at that time.

Then, one thing led to another, they were interested in the show, they got this huge new space, they wanted to have a good and popular show for the opening etc.

If you could write the ultimate history of Game Art, which artworks in the exhibition would you choose as good examples what Game Art was all about?
-Well, all of them, of course.;) I actually think there were not a lot of really great pieces that came afterwards. Game Art turned into this nerdy subgenre of media art, and kind of disappeared from my radar.
I am personally still most fond of the pieces by Jodi, especially these hacked Basic Games, officially titled "Jet Set Willy © 1984" (2002), but that is of course, because I had a hand in them being commissioned. I did a show with Jodi for Annette Schindler. Who ran the Basel-based art space Plug-In, and apart from showing older work, they did these pieces for the show. The show travelled to Berlin and to New York later, and it my proudest accomplishment among the few exhibitions that I did. It is a hard-sell for the audience, because it is about this really arcane and dated technology, and you have to be a bit of a geek to truly appreciate it. Then again, it was to me among the most "pure" works of game art because they worked with games, that allowed for very fundamental changes, because the code was so primitive and completely open. Anyway, Jodi for me always did the most representative and long-lasting works in whatever medium they worked, whether it was the net, computer interfaces, browsers, or now Google maps. They really have staying power, and they are still around, you really have to admire them for their creativity, their stamina, their will power and their stubbornness.
But, again, I think all the pieces in the show were good, and I think the show is still a very representative overview over some of the best game art works. And I think that it really made the show appealing, that it was not just works from the "usual suspects" but that it also had works from people that are not really part of that scene, like Yang Zhenzhong or Aurélien Froment.

There were some pieces, that should have been in the show, but were not for different reasons, like "Museum Meltdown" by Tobias Bernstrup and Palle Torrson because of its historic significance and "Pencil-Whipped" by Lonnie Flickinger for its sheer outlandishness.

As a media art theorist writing about net.art and Game Art how would you place Game Art in a contemporary art context?
-Again, Game Art for me as a genre started to look exhausted after we had done the show. I am not really up to date what is going on in this field recently, so I should be careful with my opinions.
Nevertheless I think it is safe to say that Game Art never really reached the contemporary art context, at least if you talk about art that is sold in the art market. There were a few artists, like Feng Mengbo, who for some time got shown in regular galleries and even in Documenta, but in the long run, it just did not get any lasting recognition at all.
That goes not only for Game Art, but also net art and Software art, and I have raved and ranted elsewhere extensively about this, so I do not want to get into it again, but I think it has to do with some kind of technophobia in the art scene, the fact that the art scene is much more commercially driven than it was in the 70s, when video art became first successful and the fact that this kind of works has this whole infrastructure of festivals etc, so artists are not really forced to interact with the "real" art world. In general, I do not mind, as I am not an art person, but was in fact much happier with the workshops for kids at the hArtware show and the fact that very ordinary people were able to relate to the works. But I still think that people like Jodi did not get what they deserved so far.
In the particular case of Game Art one aspect that does not apply to other digital art forms so much is that is really very much a work with existing games, so it most of the time ends up being some sort of appropriation art or another and often is very much about the restrictions that certain games impose on you...

Looking into the future, do you think Game Art will be eventually absorbed into the broader Artworld as one genre / format / medium / style among many others, or will it continue to exist and

45

grow somehow autonomously, with a specific set of aesthetics, theories, and practices?

-I moved to Asia in 2004, not long after the hArtware show, and I am really not so in touch with the whole media art scene anymore, but from what I perceive here, the whole scene seems a bit dead. In fact, I was surprised that somebody would still be passionate enough about the whole thing to do an interview on this show. And to learn from "Gamescenes" that there are still artists working like that.

It seems right now the focus in the art world is really on selling very traditional works for very inflated prices, and since there are known issues with turning digital art into a commodity, there is little interest in these works. So I do not see Game Art being absorbed into anything, as long as there is no "conceptual turn" in the art world at large. Who knows, maybe people will get tired of this art market art at one point. I think it is now more important than ever for artists in contemporary technology, as it is such an important and transformative aspect of global culture. But it is very risky, and I can see why not a lot of people are trying it. Sorry to disappoint you there.

I also think - and I was thinking that even back when we did the hArtware show - that the real revolution are not the artists games (actually I like this term much better than Game Art), but the original computer games themselves. I would really like to do a show on those, and have approached countless institutions about it, but so far nobody ever took me up on it. But that is something I would still like to do very very very much...

The interview took place in January of 2010.

Sylvia Eckermann: "Hotel Synthifornia" (1998)

In 1998, Sylvia Eckermann and Mathias Fuchs participated in the exhibition "Synreal: The Unreal Modification" (1998), curated by Konrad Becker, at Public Netbase in Austria. Their work "Hotel Synthifornia" a modified Unreal level, is described as a mix between the interiors of Stanley Kubrick's movie "The Shining" and the music from the Eagles's legendary song "Hotel California".

How did you get involved with the exhibition? Did you have any previous connection with Public Netbase?
- In the 90th Public Netbase was one of the most interesting and important places for digital culture in Vienna respectively in Austria. Konrad Becker and his team were not only responsible for the very first email and web accounts of many artists and people working in the field of art, they also supported the discourse of a critical and contemporary approach to new technologies. The conferences, talks, exhibitions held by Public Netbase where always on the cutting edge of what was going on in media art and theories. So, it was the place to be – for me too.

Was this the first time you worked with a videogame as a medium for artistic expression?
- When I was invited to take part in the game art exhibition "Synreal" I was very excited. I had no clue how to use a game engine or whether it could serve as an artistic tool. I couldn't claim for myself to have been a gamer either. And – I had never heard before that there was a comparable exhibition in Europe. I think it must have been one of the first of its kind. During this time I was working with Mathias Fuchs on audio-visual installations that had a strong link to to spatial conditions. The engagement with space has always been the very first step of my concepts for immersive, interactive environments. I immediately got trapped when I got in touch with the "world editor" of the first person shooter "Unreal". For weeks I could hardly leave my computer and became totally, 'addicted'. The "indoctrinator" was Max Moswitzer who was already pretty much into the techniques of game modification. He

had a very important role because most of the invited artist then had little knowledge of Computer Game Modding – but some of them are still involved in Game Art. In my earlier works of spatial electronic art and media architecture I was confronted with given qualities and conditions that for me served as frameworks. By using a Game Engine this framework went through a complete shift. The space was no longer the given starting point – it didn't exist – instead there was a huge "something" from which I could carve out any kind of "space". By pressing the "play" button, I – respectively my digital embodied appearance – could immediately experience the environment I had just now created. No SGI-machines, no expensive computers where needed to create a 3D-virtual world that moves with you in real-time. I worked a lot with digital images and digital video – now I had a tool to explore the 3rd dimension.

What is the key idea behind "Hotel Synthifornia"? The music plays obviously a crucial role in this work.
- At a flea market, we found an old record by accident: the Eagles' "Hotel California". There is this line in the song: "You can check out any time you like, but you can never leave" – somehow that reminded me of the state I was in and the spaces I made. Spaces that only lead to other spaces but never to an exit. We decided to create a kind of Hotel – as in Stanley Kubrick's movie "Shining" – with endless corridors and rooms, elevators, staircases and a pool on the lower floor. Everything was covered with seamless textures that were reminiscent of these wallpaper ornaments of the 70th. Mathias had the idea to install an old synthesizer in each room that could be triggered and one could then listen to the characteristic tunes of each machine. So we called the Level "Hotel Synthifornia".

How did the audience react to your work?
- Games are now acknowledged as culturally significant, generally speaking, comparable to film or television. But back in the 90ies people considered videogames as an activity for nerds or children and even today many still think that way although there is immense theoretical discourse at universities, conferences and in the public media. I still have the feeling that whenever I tell somebody that I

48

am an artist who does art installations with the use of Game Engines people react with astonishment. Personally I think that one reasons for this is that I'm not young, I'm female and I do not fulfill their imagination of such a persona. But the main reason was that most people had no idea what I was talking about. Of cause that has changed.

After the "Synreal" exhibition you continued to work with videogames in works as "FluID - arena of identities", "Expositur" and "Femcity"? What did you find in videogames that you couldn't find in other medium".
- For the "Synreal" exhibition in 1998 I did my very first work with a Game Engine – I knew that there was a lot more to learn, to research and to experiment with and that I just got to know and see the tip of an iceberg. For me the possibilities seemed boundless, if you had the knowhow. At that time you had to look for the expertise in all the numerous forums in the internet and you found yourself sharing your interests with mainly young, male kids all over the world. There was something new – something you couldn't find in books or learn in a university course – that was quite thrilling and challenging. I invested a lot of time to learn how to use and modify the "Unreal" Game Engine for my purposes. I had to broaden my skills in 3D-design and I had to understand at least a little bit of the language – which was something between C++ and Java – in order to not need to ask a programmer for every little detail. And the more I found out the more I was sure that this it is my artistic tool for the next years. I started each project with a greater library of scripts, textures, animations and characters. But as "Unreal" released new versions that were not convertible to the previous ones my libraries were not very useful. I thought that it is not a good idea to depend on the ideas of the game industry. So I bought my own Game Engine, a license of a professional application that allows me to build up my own structure. If you invest a lot of time into something you really have to think whether you stop or continue. After ten years I still use Game Engines but it is not satisfying any more to be engaged solely with the virtual world. My interests are still in space and its perception, in interactivity and

immersive environments, in the real and the virtual space. But I try to work out ways where both worlds interlink and merge. One example is "The Trend Is Your Friend!" 2009 (MKL, Kunsthaus Graz, Gerald Nestler, Peter Szely, Technical University of Graz) an artistic translation of a futures trading pit where I tried to make the body and mind split visible by a horizontal membrane. People wore LED-devices on their heads and had to slip through an opening in the membrane. They could only use head movements and voice to interact with a 24 meter projection that dealt with financial markets and the idea of markets in general.

You have been working with videogames for a long time and thus you have a full understanding of their history and evolution in the Game Artworld. What do you think of the future for the videogame medium as an artistic tool?
- Meanwhile there are many universities with special courses for game design all over the world; art universities are also providing courses. There are more and more huge exhibitions dealing with Game Art and even galleries have begun showing this kind of work. There are institutions that deliver the theoretical backgrounds and – today there is a generation of fathers and mothers that have been played computer games themselves. This new media is not new anymore. It has become an inherent part of a worldwide contemporary culture called Game Art.

The interview took place in February 2010.

Josephine Starrs: "Bio Tek Kitchen" (1999)

In 1999, Josephine Starrs & Leon Cmielewski developed an artistic modification of Bungie's first-person shooter Marathon titled "Bio Tek Kitchen". The modification was originally presented at "Cracking the Maze", a seminal exhibition curated by Anne-Marie Schleiner.

Was "Bio Tek Kitchen" your first game-based artistic intervention?
-I made "Bio Tek Kitchen" in 1999 with Leon Cmielewski, my collaborator on several media art projects. Before that, in the early 1990's I was a founding member of VNS Matrix, who launched the Cyberfeminist movement with our Cyberfeminist Manifesto for the 21st Century, and explored the language and structure of the early computer games in our artworks. As cited by Rachel Greene in her book Internet Art, our artwork predated the vogue for game art. We began by making up game narratives around our female protagonist All New Gen. This was before Lara Croft, when no-one thought it was possible to have a female hero in a computer game. We created game stills for light boxes, narrative sound and video works and interactive art installations. We received enormous positive feedback from young women, both gamers and non-gamers from many parts of the world. It became obvious that loads of women were really pissed off with being actively excluded from game culture and were doing something about it.

In "Bio Tek Kitchen"', the player is attacked in a kitchen by mutant vegetables engineered by a ruthless corporation whose only purpose is to take over the entire food chain. The player has to defend himself with the aid of weapons such as dish cloths and egg flippers... Do you think the videogames could be an effective means to tackle serious issues, for example the genetic modification of crops?
- Yes, why not? Humour and play have always been strategies that artists have employed in their work to create meaning; the Surrealists for example. Digital gaming has become as much of a cultural force in our world as cinema. In the same way that experimental film and video has grown alongside the mainstream

film industry, game art has emerged in the past two decades, often drawing on digital game concepts, formats and narrative structure. Themes such as war, biotechnology, the cyborg, and dystopian futures are common themes in mainstream games. I don't think any subject should be off-limits to media artists.

Leon Cmielewski and I created Seeker an interactive video installation that was playful in that it encouraged participants to map their own family migration history. It also explored relationships between conflict commodities like tantalum, which power our mobile culture, and the tragic deaths of people seeking asylum in new countries. This is an important artwork that won an Award of Distinction at Ars Electronica in 2007.

"Bio Tek Kitchen" has been showed around the world since 1999. Was the programming challenging?

-We have made many interactive works over the years, documented on our website. We maintain former hardware and software systems to support our artworks. Unfortunately museums in Australia are not interested in collecting and archiving this kind of work yet. "Bio Tek Kitchen" is a Marathon Infinity mod and runs on Macintosh OS9, so it can only easily be seen as a short machinima we made called "Kitchen Carnage".

Australia was among the earliest catalysts for Game Art. Aside from your work, one cannot forget Rebecca Cannon's seminal Select Parks or ground-breaking modifications and "indie" projects, like "Escape from Woomera". Why?

-Australia has always been very hip when is comes to new media art. We are often early adopters of new technologies, but we are also innovators and are not afraid to critique the establishment. Who knows, that irreverence could be the influence of our Indigenous culture, and perhaps the Irish convict culture.

One thing that struck me is that several Game Art pioneers are women. It surprises me for at least two reasons. One, because Game Art is a niche genre in contemporary art. Second, in the mid-

Nineties there were relatively few women playing or developing videogames, unlike today...
-One reason for this is that the games industry ignored women and girls for more than a decade, perhaps fearing that if they market games to girls the boys would be unhappy about losing their no-girl zone. So even though women were often excluded from the mainstream game industry, female artists could have fun making their own games, hacking the game engines, slashing the dominant game narratives and critiquing the content and structure of mainstream game culture.

Do you believe that Game Artists specifically, and, in general, artists working with videogames have somehow contributed to a broader socio-cultural acceptance of videogames as an artistic medium?
- Yes, to a certain extent. There are many games that are great works of art, but it might take a new generation of art curators to convince our cultural institutions of that. Also, mainstream culture has always had a history of taking ideas from artists for commercial gain no matter what the medium. And artists love mashing up mainstream culture to create fantastic art.

The interview took place in March 2010.

Margarete Jahrmann: "Synreal exhibition" (1999)

In 1995 Max Moswitzer and Margarete Jahrmann launched Konsum Arts_Server, by setting up a Linux server connected to a local network of servers in Vienna. The Konsum Arts Server is today the host for works as LinX3D a 3rdWeb MultiUser game on ASCII loginfiles datavatars. Jahrmann's interest for Game Art was first discovered, as many other artists, at the Synreal exhibition in 1999.

When did you start playing videogames? And why did you decide to use them for your artistic interventions?
- Well when I was still at school, playing with my first computer- that was in the mid 80ies.... The first game which impressed me was a black and white game- for Macintosh called Cosmic Osmo. It was a sweet alien, aesthetically, appealing and clever- reminded me of comics. Well in terms of gameplay I liked Shuffle Puck at this time – nice relaxing reaction booster. The switch to work with games was later. In 1999 I created the first game engine modification - which was then exhibited at the Synreal show in Vienna and other places

The "Synreal: The Unreal Modification" (1999) exhibition was the starting point for many artists experimenting with Game Art. Can you tell me some about your experience?
-I started artistically to work with games with Synreal. The game I made - was called "superfem" sth. It was playing with textures of different operating systems and aimed to establish a sort of "identity" by showing the login screen surfaces of the machine you started your application on. It was quite sophisticated already- involving multiuser- based on Unreal engine. For example if you came from a Unix system, or Windows or Macintosh system you could shoot your surface on to others. Synreal was a very rich experience- especially one night when we invited non art people for a tournament- to play in artists levels. I was moderating live on stage, like in a boxing ring, this night together with Hans Wu, a Viennese journalist, who with his Asiatic long hair looked like a real game nerd. It was an interesting experience that players said artists levels are unplayable ;) Later I made LinX3D in collaboration with

Max Moswitzer. This was then integrating the question of the Interface already- exhibiting it with a retro style console- because we noted the problem of the adequate exhibition mode for game based works.

Your artworks have been displayed in several European museums and galleries for the past ten years. Did you notice a change in attitude toward Game Arts? Are critics and visitors reacting differently to your ludic artworks today compared to the early days of Game Art?

-Museums need certain logics of arts and public display to be fulfilled. But for me this was always a positive challenge - to quit the boring pure virtuality and to make it more dirt by integrating the physical body, the art coded installation. Ars Electronia at OK Center Linz in 2003 was a very great opportunity- we built a player generated architecture of a shooter game- only the carved out shapes in human size- a complete room of about 60 square meters was filled with that- that was wonderful!

Also the experience at V2 lab Rotterdam at the Las Palmas exhibition space and at Gallery Mama in 2003/04 was perfect. We also had the opportunity to build a circular screen of about 12 meters for a real immersive experience - combined with a living room situation...to seduce players to send out anti-war mails by shooting. ... and showed an art coded print out of the game architecture- the generative architecture of course - in a vitrina like a modern sculpture.

So the attitude of the art public and critics was that Game Art was hard to understand for both sides-because gamers were surprised that we were still working within the logics of arts and in the arts world it was still not recognised as art work and appeared as too nerdy. Maybe today that has changed- I don't know. The last show was in Aarhus in a big museum AROS- and it was a gamework- among classical media arts works- and was at least received very well by a big audience.

Today you work as a professor of Game Design at Zurich University of Arts. One thing that strikes me is that many of the artists who

started to work with Game Art in the mid-Nineties today work at universities with videogames. Why?
-I think this is quite normal.... because due to market mechanisms only a few people can deal with art market. The playfulness is the main focus of insight- a method from my point of view. This is expressed in works as the very recent "toygenosonic". Urban Plays as interventionist art play critically address the surveillance dimension of electromagnetic topographies in present time's urban space. The "invisible city", which is in the sense of Italo Calvino (1974) a narrative lived space, becomes a materialist topic and play field. While users were playing a game in urban space, namely those of competing to each other who would find the most accessible hot spots in an urban environment and documenting this by a photo, the awareness about the invisible topography layered over the existing visible city was made clear. A side effect of political explosiveness was the fact that by entering and scanning such points each player leaves traces. This was not topic of urban play as Objects of Desire 2008, Blitz Play Bergen 2007 and Toygenosonic 2009, which were realised with different collaborators under the label Ludic Society. However the mentioned arts projects have in common, that also a non-art audience is touched by the performances and play in public space, networked media, where the dissemination of the play takes place.

Tell me about the Nybble-Engine project. It reminds me of The Matrix, an engine whose goal is to showcase the hidden information of the net and construct architecture made of bits...
-Yes - you got it pretty well. But in our case it was not ONLY textures- it was really a total conversion of the engine, which fully integrated commandos of a Linux server as working function into an game engine. So your REALLY could start commandos from inside the game - as NS look up traceroute, send mail, receive mail- only by shooting or bumping into objects.
We introduced a second text layer, which displayed all that feature live in real-time inside the engine. This was developed during a three month residency at the V2lab in Rotterdam and supported by them.

Where would you say that Game Art stands today?
- Well - it is more integrated into art world may be - young artists quickly get invited into shows, if they label their work as "game art" - and then parallel also designer games are more art like nowadays. There is a whole strain of authors who creates mini games which are award winning - this is a big difference to the team work based big games. I don't see the return of the author very positive in this concern. I am a too old fashioned idealist artist I know ;)

The interview took place in March 2010.

Robert Nideffer: "The Tomb Raider Patch" (1999)

Robert Nideffer is a professor of Studio Art and Informatics; Co-Director for the Art, Computation and Engineering Program (ACE), Director of the UC Irvine Game Culture and Technology Lab and Affiliated faculty in the Visual Studies Program.

In 1999 you took part in the seminal exhibition "Cracking the Maze". For that event, you developed a now legendary patch forTomb Raider. Can you tell me something about the exhibition, how you got involved, and if you had earlier experiences with videogame-based art?

- As you probably know, the exhibition was curated by Anne-Marie Schleiner, a very interesting artist in her own right. It was the first online specifically game-art focused exhibit I'm aware of. I found her concept really interesting. If memory serves correct, she put out some sort of call and I responded to it, and she wa gracious enough to let me do something for the show. At that point I'd certainly played a lot of videogames, and had been doing some work that either had elements of games in it and/or was inspired by games, but it wasn't really the main focus of much of the work in the way it's become ove the past 10+ years since. For example I'd done my Ph.D. in the social sciences a few years earlier ("Bodies, Nobodies, and Antibodies At War: Operation Desert Storm and the Politics of the "Real"", 1994) as an interactive CD-ROM dealing with the mediation of the Gulf War of '91. The role that the trope of "gaming" played in that project was a pretty big part of the analysis, as was inclusion of actual game media that was being produced at the time, and which was part of the general "discursive terrain" of the war effort so to speak, not to mention all the wargame simulation Genral "Stormin' Norman" Schwarzkopf was using to prep soldiers for the battlefield down in Florida. Post Ph.D., as an MFA student, I got the chance to production manage and art-direct another CD-ROM project in collaboration with the noted physicist Stephen Hawking called "Life in the Universe" which, in addition to the overall UI being pretty playful and game-like, incorporated a couple of Director based games - one to replicate RNA sequences, and another to decode radio signals, inspired by Hawking's liking and suport of the Search for Extra Terrestrial Intelligence (SETI) Institute's mission. Other than that, it was mostly just little hacks and experiments for fun.

What was the intention behind the Tomb Raider patch? It played a very influential role in the history of Game Art.
- Ummm, well I'm not sure I would dare claim it as such, but gee, thanks! The theme of Schleiner's show was the game "hack," "patch," or "crack." In that context the crack became a means to reflect on gaming culture from another angle, and to attempt to contribute to the formation of new configurations of game characters, game space, and gameplay. At the time of the show, the real Tomb Raider (published by Eidos Interactive), and its main heroine Lara Croft, was an extremely popular video game franchise. So popular in fact, it had become the target of one of the most famous underground game patches called "Nude Raider," which stripped the title character of what little clothes she had. I decided I wanted to "patch the patch" for my project. In that interest, Tomb Raider consisted of three-parts: 1) an appropriated website where I repurposed the existing commercial site; 2) a spoofed mail-server that re-routed messages submit to her fan club website to the Director of development at Eidos UK as if it were coming from the Director of Marketing in the US branch; and 3) a patched version of the Nude Raider patch, which placed police blotter style bar codes across Lara's private parts (and gave her a goatee as a Duchampian homage), thwarting the game player's expectation of seeing her polygonal private parts.

Did people back them "get" this particular artwork? I mean, it paid homage to Duchamp's "L.H.O.O.Q", but in a videogame context. However, if the viewer was not familiar with the original artifact or did not have a clue about Lara Croft, she/he was bound to miss out on a significant part of the artwork.
-Well, comprehension is always an issue, isn't it. There's certainly plenty of times, after it's all said and done, that I'm not even sure I unterstand what my work's about. Usually I just try to make up

compelling enough stories after the fact - for merit and promotion, for interviews, or simply for my own need to feel I've done something worthwhile with my time! Seriously though, you're absolutely right, and such things as tongue in cheek (or van-dyke on chin) nods to Duchamp, or my patch's relationship to the original Nude Raider patch for example, are often easily lost in the mix. I remember one critical review written where the piece was mentioned and the author, though she was quite flattering (and an extremely smart theorist), interpreted the piece in a completely unexpected way - and certainly not one I'd thought much about when making it. That's not to say it wasn't a perfectly valid reading, it was just comprehension of another sort. So I guess all I'm trying to say is that "getting it" is a tricky game, and often has little if any to do with authorial intent, goals, and objectives - that can be the beauty and/or the horror of it.

The following year you organized an equally important exhibition with Antoinette LaFarge titled "SHIFT-CTRL". What was the idea behind this event? And why was it held at The Beall Center for Art and Technology?
- "SHIFT-CTRL" was the inaugural exhibition for the Beall Center for Art and Technology, then a brand new media art facility at the University of California Irvine campus. It was one of the first international exhibitions to showcase the use of game metaphors, design principles, and technologies as part of a critical art practice. We felt this was particularly important to do as games exploded from a niche market dominated by a youth demographic to occupy cultural center stage. The exhibition showcased a broad array of creative work related to gaming, and provided alternative models for looking at how computer games and gaming culture were affecting the larger society. We had a pretty good budget, so we could do it right. The show was supported by Rockwell International, the Beall Family Foundation, RareCSP, Attachmate Corporation, Antenna Design New York Inc., Apple, and Toshiba America. The works were clustered into three main conceptual categories: "role-playing games as shared social spaces," "evolvable and emergent systems, "and "world hacks." "SHIFT-CTRL" was

pretty well received, and got coverage in a variety of media including the LA Times, OC Register, OC Weekly, GameFace Magazine, NPR, and PBS affiliate KOCE-TV. The Beall Center was, interestingly enough, endowed by Donald Beall who was the retired Chairman and CEO of the Rockwell Corporation - a transnational corporation renowned for manufacture of electronic controls and communications, particularly in the fields of avionics, munitions, and manufacturing. However, Mr. Beall is credited with streamlining Rockwell's management program, and steering the company away from its dependence on the defense industry to focus on commercial electronics. My understanding was he gave the grant to UCI as a gift to his wife Joan, who had been very active in promoting K-12 arts education in Orange County. Apparently, rumor has it, they at least liked the show! In general it was very well received by the campus, the surrounding community, and the media - which was great, since it was a bit of a risk at the time. People came from all over the Southern California region (and beyond) to see it. Lots more kids and families came than was expected and/or usual for art shows on campus, teachers brought classes on field trips, etc. We were pretty pleased with how popular it was while up.

How would you describe the North-American Game Art scene a decade ago? Was there any interest in Iodo-artistic interventions or was digital gaming largely ignored in artistic contexts?
- Well, it still can be hard to convince some people that videogames can be art objects. But it remains equally hard to convince them that urinals can be art objects too! Convincing people what should or shouldn't count as art is as at least as thorny a problem as comprehension. I remember soon after coming to the UCI campus (around the time-frame you mention, or maybe a little before), I gave a talk to a group of very smart people from all over campus interested in information technology, computing, HCI, social theory, and so on. At the end of my presentation, which included a number of game-related projects, the first question I got asked was "Well that's all very interesting, but what makes it art?" Not missing a beat (I suppose because such a response was not entirely

unexpected) I queried back "Because I'm in the art department?" At least they laughed. But to try to respond more directly to your question, my sense at the time was that, at least in terms of the people I was dealing with which included other artists (as well as colleagues from a variety of other disciplinary locales), critics, historians, the general public, were quite curious about what was going on, and the fact that it was happening in within a "fine art" frame of reference didn't seem to be an issue. If it was, I never heard about it.

Looking back at the early years of Game Art, is there anything that you find surprising about the evolution of Game Art?
- It's certainly been exciting to watch how much it's grown, and how sophisticated and facile new generations of artists are in working with the medium, both technically as well as conceptually, particularly those who come out of a strong critically informed background and training in the arts. It's also been interesting to watch various cultural institutions - galleries, museums, universities, just to name a few - have made moves to embrace game inspired art, culture, and technology. My sense is that many people and places are struggling to make sense of and situate what's happening "on the ground." That struggle often reflects a variety of mixed motives - i.e., games being presented as "art" as a way of bringing more bodies through museum doors, courting resource-rich games companies into sponsoring cultural events by framing their visual components of their product as fine art, game-centered academic programs being developed to boost flagging enrollments in certain disciplines and/or to try to get corporate kick-backs, and so on. But those mixed motives, and the attempted sense-making, is a big part of what keeps it interesting. I just wish I could be around 50 years from now to see what's going on.

The interview took place in March 2010.

Carlo Zanni: "Average Shoeveler" (2004)

"Carlo Zanni was born in La Spezia (Italy) in 1975. Since the early 2000's his practice involves the use of Internet data to create time based social consciousness experiences investigating our life. Zanni's practice finds its roots in Sol Lewitt's artist statement, 'The idea becomes a machine that makes the art', which he translates into a contemporary adaptation, 'The idea becomes the code that renders the art.'" from the artist's homepage

The videogame Average Shoveler" (2004) evokes the look-and-feel of a classic adventure such as Leisure Suit Larry I (1987). What is your relationship to Leisure Suit Larry? Are there other games that have inspired you? What kind of influences can we expect in your future works?
- I was playing that game during my early high school years. A friend of mine brought these black floppies and a bunch of paper sheets in English that listed all the shortcuts to reach the end of the game.
To me it was an epiphany. I don't usually play games. I'd love to do it but I don't know why I never do it. I've played The Sims, the very first series. I've played Indiana Jones & The Last Crusade at the same time of Leisure Suit Larry. Test Drive, Flight Simulator and some example of primordial soccer games.
I remember buying a lot of magazines about videogames but not playing that much.
Now I remember I played a lot of tennis on a Nintendo box in the Nineties when I spent one year doing social services instead of joining the army. Hours and hours.

"Average Shoveler" was commissioned by Rhizome at the New Museum. How did that come to be?
- Rhizome launched the program in 2001 and my work was awarded a commission in 2004:
"For the 2004-05 cycle, artists were invited to submit proposals relating to the theme of games. The call asked artists to propose projects that will contribute to the art game genre, or reflect on

broad interpretations of the word "game." from Rhizome homepage.

"Average Shoveler" reminds me a bit of Space Invaders: it doesn't matter how good you are at shooting down aliens or shovelling snow, you just can't win. Can you tell me something about the idea behind your game – and its embedded failure system?
- I thought Space Invaders had an end, a goal to reach. Perhaps the destruction of the big spaceship? Anyway, they are two very different things. "Average Shoveler" doesn't have points or levels or goals. It is a delivery system for "breaking news" masqueraded as a videogame. It's our daily intellectual spoon of white phosphorus bombs for total brainwashing. It is obviously a fictional environment but the feedback you get while playing is completely real: it stinks, it is a thick and sticky runway of blood and you catwalk on it, tapping your slick keyboard. On one level, "Average Shoveler" is quite boring: it turns into a contemplative screen when you get into the buildings and find yourself in a surreal scenario. On another, it is always morphing and changing, thus offering you unexpected adventures. But you need to do some extra work, think about what you're experiencing. It's not your average mind numbing videogame. It's tomorrow seen from today. The fun comes when you realize the implications behind the gameplay, and this takes some time and intellectual effort.

You are familiar with both the Italian and the North American art scene. Do you see any difference between the two countries in terms of critical reception, openness to experimentations etc.?
-If a critic approaches your work seriously it doesn't really matter if he is Italian or American. There are cultural differences of course, but these details are irrelevant, almost invisible. The real problem has to do with the large number of curators, critics, and dealers that have no background in new media: they don't give a shit, they just don't "get it", and because they don't understand, your work has no value whatsoever. They don't even ask the artist because admitting their ignorance would compromise their "expertise". Therefore, if you're working with new media – especially with videogames and

internet art – you basically don't exist, you're not even on the radar. Occasionally you see a bunch of shows that feature a few media pieces, but usually not in mainstream galleries or museums. It is a fringe-like business. You don't see new media works regularly shown in important group shows around the globe like it happens with other media, like photography, video, painting, and installations, nor you find them at top art fairs. In auctions, videos sell next to nothing in comparison to other media. Paul Pfeiffer, Bill Viola, Doug Aitken, Pipilotti Rist, Gary Hill, Tony Oursler who else? Think of the current paradox: there are millions of people right now creating videos with their cell phones but the bottom line is that the market still only trusts a piece of paper with ink on it. This is a problem for game Art and new media art. I guess the real question is: Can auctions related to new media art work the same way as auctions for paintings and traditional art? The above artists can sell their pieces as installations and/or hardware with embedded videos. I still have some doubts that a video can make $100.000+ in an auction in the form of a burned DVD with a signature on it, at least if not done hundred years ago: time is a gentleman in regard to history but not very often in regard to living people. The North American art scene is wider and broader. In some ways, it's easier to get attention and opportunities to exhibit your work. Also, American universities are always eager to embrace new subjects and have been always investing in research while in Italy everything happens at a slow, glacial pace. Italy is paradoxically doomed by its Past and Tradition, both a bless and a burden. Other factors that prevent to country to explore new territories are the pervasiveness of the politics of the Church and the equally toxic popularity of neorealism and arte povera. At the same time, Europe as a whole provides plenty of opportunities for artists that do not fit the established canons. Moreover, there are smart minded curators who are able to recognize new phenomena, but like the artists themselves, they face similar problems in surviving in a conservative artworld. No matter how hard you try, if you work with games, you are pretty much invisible in the establishment of art. This is an important point to make because the artworld is a place where money comes and goes very fast. For these very reasons, it is an interesting playground. The hardest one. Nevertheless, for artists like us, ignored by the high powers of Art, Steve Jobs's words come to mind as an inspiration, or better, as an imperative: This ain't just business, This is practically spiritual... This is about overthrowing dead culture. Dead gods.

Antonio Riello's "Italiani Brava Gente" is one of the earliest examples of Italian Game Art. What is your relationship to that artwork? Can you name any artists that inspired your investigation?
- "Italiani Brava gente" is a masterpiece. I came in contact with this artwork relatively late, in 1999, I don't remember. Around that time, I discovered an easy way to create simple videogames and I was experimenting with the possibilities of making art using a game-like structure. It took me a lot of effort and it did not quite work until Average Shoveler. As for the second part of your question, usually I don't find myself inspired by other visual artists' works but at the same time, there are some seminal pieces that I feel very close to, for many reasons. Among others, I would mention Cory Arcangel's "Landscape Study" (2002); Yucef Merhi's "Atari Poetry I" (2001); Jon Haddock's "Isometric Screenshots" (2000); Mauro Ceolin's RGB Tetris (2002) and Marco Brambilla's "HalfLife (Surveillance Channel)" (2002).

What is the relationship between videogames and art?
-There's clearly a parallel between Game Art/Video Art and the videogame industry/film industry. With the introduction of inexpensive camcorders in the Eighties, many artists began to experiment with the new format and video art boomed. Clearly, these videos were (and are) much smaller in production size than the average Hollywood production. The distribution and worldwide success of videogames created a gigantic industry of multi-million dollar titles (both in terms of budget and revenue). Tools like Flash and screen capture applications as well as hacking techniques are helping artists to craft game-like projects. Like art videos, these are usually smaller in size than their counterparts for the mass market. But things are changing: think about the emergence of DIY film-

making, epitomized by films such as "Breaking Upwards" or "Paranormal Activities" that cost about $15.000 to make. Filmmakers are exploring new formats and tools to create feature films. And the studios are taking notice: Paramount, for instance, is opening a new division called Insurge Pictures to "micro finance" up to ten movies with a maximum budget of $100.000 each. The repercussions on video art will be huge and the might amplify the very meaning of terms like DIY, which too often refers to lo-fi, rough, crude, and – let's admit it – juvenile, crappy projects. We might see something similar with Art Games that could feature much longer and much more complex narratives...

What can videogames do for the art scene?
-Going abstract, I can say that a pivotal feature of videogames is the chance to save the game you are playing with. You stop playing and come back on it even days later. It is much more like when you read a book or you follow a TV series. This is interesting to me because there is a time while you rest your mind; you think of your past experience, you sort of meditate on it. Perhaps you feel some sort of a urge growing inside, a wish that needs to be fulfilled in your next play. I would like to see this approach transferred to the art scene, where too many people are just jumping from a project to the next, trusting their own taste but never looking outside their courtyard, so to speak. This is another problem within the artworld that is promoting and presenting to the audience very easy decorative works or modernist revivals. Game Art could challenge the status quo.

The interview took place in April 2010.

Joan Leandre: "retroYou" (1999-2004)

"In 1999 he developed some software reversing techniques using commercial digital-distraction products such as computer games resulting in the series retroyou RC Fuck the Gravity Code, retroyou RC Butterfl y Overfl ow and retroyou nostal(G) phoenix West. Some unfi nished projects are Deep Boot and the long ongoing series retroyou nostalg2. Other collective projects include the Babylon Archives and Velvet Strike." from the transmediale.de homepage

In 2004, you took part in the Whitney Biennial as a member of the "The Velvet-Strike team", which also featured Anne-Marie Schleiner and Brody Condon. How did this collaboration come to be? What was the idea behind "Velvet-Strike"?
- We met somehow with Anne Marie in Barcelona. Anne's work was sort of a reference to me, same with Brody. I think there was a lot of mutual understanding and coincidence in what we all many people were doing, after all, this sort of complicity is what makes a team project go on by itself, in a natural way...and it's the same for any good thing in life, good stuff goes out the easy way, the rest is just wrong. No need for additives.
After the events in 2001 we somehow decided to break into one of those simwar networks and "Counter Strike" was one of the more visible and popular and so to speak iconic computer distraction productions related to this "fight against terrorism" nonsense fear vs horror god damned nightmare. We proposed a public contest for making anti-war graffiti inside the game using some native features of the software. There was later a replica of the "Counter Strike" web site from where you could download those mods and use them in your own system. Suddenly this crazy guys "playing" counter strike could see those naif and cheese anti-war graffiti in the walls of the game where they were trying to kill the "bad" boys. In my opinion Velvet Strike was an attempt to put in crisis the term "game" when applied to such a thing, that is when the so called game crosses the boundary of the act of playing itself and goes become some sort of narcotic routine for bewildered people. I mean when the natural process of learning is gone from the act of

playing and you go spend your life in the screen triggering digital events in the machine. Velvet Strike was about using the native possibilities of the software to reverse its own meaning inside a social network. It was about inducing some feedback inside this community of so to speak "players" and suggest the possibility to scape the routine of such monochromatic psychopath after all lonely practices. Then, calling it art or something else is beyond the content of the project itself, that was in my opinion just an aftermath which was good for starting a debate and a public knowledge about the topic.

At the Whitney Biennal 2004 Cory Arcangel's seminal "Super Mario Cloud" was also on display. It's curious that two game-based art projects were selected that year, isn't it?

- In the mid to late 90's there was a first wave of people being interest in bringing computer game software productions beyond the standards of entertainment and distraction and do something else whatever we would like to call it, from simple jokes to more elaborated projects. Those, such as early works by Anne Marie, Brody, Julien Oliver, Eddo Stern, Jodi...we were sharing a lot with Jodi by the time around 1999 here in Barcelona when I was finishing "retroyou RC FCK the Gravity Code" and they just finished the "Untitled Game" series which is in my opinion a work of an extraordinary importance.

In those days computer games didn't get yet to the level of socialization, popularity and business of nowadays but that was just a matter of time. Few years later I think Hartware and Tilman's Games among very few other exhibits draw a line. Between 2003 and 2004 there was a peak when it comes to this interest for computer game based projects...there started to be many exhibitions and many people going into this. Nothing new actually, this is the way it works, like waves...you might be a good surfer then you spot a perfect wave you go for it you ride it and enjoy, then as wave looses power you just go down and try to catch another one, some people does love surfing.

"Velvet" and "Super Mario Clouds" were included in the Biennial because both were recent contemporary oriented and heterogeneous projects inside this new ready to exploit digital art trend category so called gameart or whatever terminology you'd like to use. I personally think this is obviously a really weak and poor approach, this waves of new fresh stuff...I don't like this social surf it's too much static monochrome but sometimes by accident you are on the wave. It works as in this mood of permanent update typical of our days specially when it comes to tech products, when today you buy some new trendy device and tomorrow becomes an insult to your dignity because is too old fashioned. It is all so obvious that better not to talk about it. In any case "Velvet Strike" started as some sort of interruption in a very particular war-sim network. It made some people inside this environment very mad and upset which means the project actually made sense. For a few months they mailed us, they insulted and told us they would kill us and so, then they invited us to Whitney and many other events, the circle was closed.

In 2003 you took part in the exhibition "Games: Computer games by artists" (11/10-30/11-2003) @ Hartware Medien Kunst Verein, Dortmund-Hörd, curated by Tilman Baumgärtel. Can you share something with us about this exhibition? How did you get involved?
- Games was a great pleasure and I have a nice memory, I worked before with Iris Dressler & Hans D. Christ at Hartware Medien Kunst Verein in a software exhibition called Control Panels, those people are always really fully involved in what they do. They did a good job together with Tilman. The exhibition as I said before was somehow the first big one about computer game based projects, it was split in two parts, as far as I remember one about software and installation projects the second one about video productions related to the computer game sphere.

In Dortmund you presented "retroYou nostal(G)" (2002-2003) which is now regarded as milestone of Game Art. Since then, you have returned to retroYou several times. That concept resurfaces in other of your works. Can you explain your iterative strategy?
- Retroyou was some sort of joke environment which hosted several serial projects. It was never intended to be a monolithic project but

a modular project. The first series was totally finished in 1999 composed of many variations starting with "retroyou RC Fck the Gravity Code" and "retroyou RC Butterfly Overflow" which was based on a very popular racing game of the late 90,s

The native main objectives of interactivity (racing-competition) and narratives in the original game were progressively vanishing after a precise act of interruption via software, someone could talk about deconstruction which at this point sounds a little obvious to me, I rather prefer to think about this sort of interventions as interruptions or even better translations. So then, the gravity center of such a simulated world was set to be spinning around so there were all floating objects, no racing, no game and progressively the software itself was turning into some sort of self running screen saver running without the need of any human input. One could float away beyond the limits of the game map, you could see all the hidden geometry, all the mess from above while getting into the blue sky...it was really like visiting the backstage of the software itself. That was a great pleasure, like finally finding something really suggestive inside a commercial computer game. I remember this fresh feeling of doing something that is sharp and simple.

The retroyou environment project continued as some sort of serialized collection of tests on different contexts not only computer games, some of them were never shown as they were not intended to be shown at all. In some sort of continuation to retroyou RC there was "retroyou nostal(G) Wings of Fire" which in few words was about a flight simulator reduced to the minimal expression, geographic data was lost, there was only one remaining airport at 3500 meters high with a runaway one square meter of size, aircraft aerodynamics turned into a crazy nightmare, no human could pilot such an aircraft, again only the machine was allowed to fly the Iron Bird. So, I could honestly say, all together is a continuity of tests based on software or in general in the contemplation and translation of mass media environments as well as about the act of interrupting them.

In general I think it is very relevant this idea of postulating against progress as it is understood by corporate powers, for instance in the form of tiny particular projects of reversing, interrupting or whatever sort of symbolical acts of sabotage. Perhaps this is very important these days. It gives us the chance to put some color in this very often monochromatic global society and to trigger some nice feedback, like a Boomerang round trip.

Could you describe your relationship to games and art?
-As you can guess I'm a cheater when it comes to technology and I never understood the technological medium in an unconditional way...basically I can't understand the tasteless euphoric approach to technology same when it comes to art, no way. Takes long slow time in life to get to learn, I never played computer games, little excess with computer is bad for health and at some point it makes you stupid. You really have to cheat if you are to survive computers. Instead of being a victim or part of the bewildered herd I choose to take a distance and put some close look to what is beyond the machine. I always felt close to the observation of mass media phenomenon's and the effort to draw an interpretation hypothesis for instance, how do they work and how the are being used. I consider "Velvet Strike" or "RC" and the rest of projects including the "Babylon Archives" or the new recent series "In the Name of Kernel", something closer to this sort of analytical approach expressed with great fury or with great calm.

The resulting object somehow might later escape your control and turn into pure art fetishism...others will like it, understand it or just write and guess about it but as said before that's another story. Basically the digital entertainment business is now in the epicenter of this galaxy of products, sub-products, fascination and repulsion, this sinister and blurry idea of progress, of data property where everything is a game of mirrors and most people get bewildered and fall into this narcotic state of mind when the screen becomes your kingdom and your body a prison. Now, this idea of game is very important for the world these days more than ever before, I mean the true game when playing is about true learning as opposite to cloning, repetition, mass production, machine slavery.

I found it was really fun to change the sense and meaning of mass media products. It was nice to cheat computer games and use them in such a way they became absurd toys. Interrupting computer games is the real playtime. Playing is a matter of freedom without conditions as it should be in art and any other human activity. By default mass media distraction computer games are designed to reproduce the conditions of slavery through the administration of regular doses of permanent updating, all covered by a layer of colorful and euphoric promises. Crowds of people are ruining their lives in the screen giving feedback to a machine which in a broader context is no more than a giant pocket calculator.

The interview took place in April 2010.

Julian Oliver: QTHOTH (1998-1999)

"Julian Oliver is a New Zealander, Critical Engineer and artist based in Berlin. His work and lectures have been presented at many museums, galleries, international electronic-art events and conferences...He is an advocate of Free and Open Source Software and is a supporter of, and contributor to, initiatives that promote and reinforce civil rights in the networked domain." from the artist's homepage

In 1998, you and Rebecca Cannon launched Selectparks which quickly became the essential repository of Game Art, documenting the most diverse artistic game-development practices. How did you embark in this project? And what is the future of the archive?
- I founded Selectparks in 1998 but it was only later, with the addition of Rebecca, that the project grew as an art-game news and archiving project. Meanwhile Chad Chatterton, myself and others were busy making game-based art under the Selectparks name.
Selectparks was initially created in the interest of drawing attention to what we, at the time, saw as an extremely unique, emerging and under-represented scene, that of truly experimental game modification and development. Back then there were really only a few artists in the world expressly working in this vein; small beginnings indeed for what is now an ever important field within contemporary art in iself.
There's been plenty of talk of taking Selectparks and producing a searchable, useful archive of all the content there - much of which isn't publically visible right now. It's just a case of time really, something that none of us have since our respective careers have taken us off in different directions.

What is in your opinion the most important/interesting Game Artwork currently available Selectparks? Why?
-That's really hard to answer! As I've never been a person to have a single favourite colour or food I'm going to have to give you three favourites.

I think "PSDoom" is right up there with the best of them. "PSDoom" maps game events (largely the shooting of Doom's monsters) onto processes running on the host operating system: what you think is a monster in the game might actually represent Mozilla Firefox, your image editor or even the process responsible for your graphical display itself. By shooting these monsters you actually terminate these processes.

This is a very early example of a game design reaching out of itself and manipulating the host, a kind of dangerous promiscuity.

"PainStation" was and still is a very important contribution to what we call game art. It lifts the abstraction of computer mediated game events, as perceived, and writes them onto the actual nervous system of the player; tearing at the skin, passing electricity into the body from the game system, bypassing the visual cortex and the emotional frustrations ubiquitous to computer gaming itself by feeding back into that which is unnegotiable in a player, their tissue, their wires. PainStation is an important cybernetic perversion/revision of the human<->machine relationship, up there with Stelarc's Ping Body and other great works of cyborgian ambition.

My final pick would be Eddo Stern's "RunnersEQ"' (1999). Acting as an intervention in the once popular MMORPG EverQuest, Eddo subjects three avatars to run across the world indefinitely, witnessed (or annoyed by) countless thousands of committed players. All they do is run.

Three computer mice - joined together such that they cannot be moved independently - control the forward direction, but not speed, of all three runners simultaneously. I see this game as example of a very early 'action', in the Situationist sense, in a multiplayer game. Brody Condon's "Worship" is in a similar vein.

For "QTHOTH" and "q3apd" you used the Quake engine to experiment with music. There were not that many artists who used FPS engines for creating music with videogames – one of the examples that comes to mind is Sylvia Eckermann and Matthias Fuchs' "Hotel Synthifornia" (1998). Today, music games have become a mainstay, an established genre, eg Guitar Hero, Singstar,

Rock Band... In a sense, you were a pioneer... Why is the combination of music and videogames so interesting to you?
- I used to make a lot of noise music and was somewhat frustrated with a performance context limited to a laptop running software like Pure Data or SuperCollider. Around 1998 I discovered that it was relatively trivial to repurpose a moddable game as an instrument in itself. This coincided three interests for me at the time: hypothetical architecture, experimental music and computer gaming. I have always conceptualised sound spatially; for me it more interesting (and convenient) to map properties like sustain, delay and pitch to events and ideas in a synthetic 3D environment than a physical sound-installation as such.

You've always used open, free software to create your artworks. In the early days, many game engines were freely available and users could modify them to create their own games/projects. In today's fiercely competitive scene, however, game companies are not so eager so share the source code of their best titles with the community. Would you say that the hacker's ethic, the ideology of open-source code was essential to the genesis of Game Art? What would have happened if Nintendo's mentality – a mentality of closenness – had prevaled in the PC market as well? How has the situation changed in the last decade? What are the ripercussions on the Game Art scene? How crucial was the open-source philosophy to your own artistic experimentation?
- I think the 'moddability' of those early engines was not just important but simply vital to the growth of the field. Having game-code exposed for manipulation and/or being able to load in custom art was seen as a creative boon for many of us. While many of us already had Amigas, development was often quite cumbersome, innaccessible for many. Being able to make such rich, complex game-based art at home on your cheap Pentium II and 64Mb of RAM really opened things up.

Over the years I became a better programmer. As my curiosity and skill-levels increased so did my need to reach beyond the interaction models, player subjectivities and other creative restrictions 'moddable' games represented: I started to ask: "Am I creating through this tool or is this tool creating through me?" I wanted access to engine source code, even to try to implement whole games myself working from code libraries found online.

Linux based operating systems were a big deal for me in this regard, and still are. I've learnt a huge amount from reading other people's source code, beyond game engines themselves. I realised it was possible to 'glue' just about anything to anything else, to arrive at truly weird and unusual outcomes. It was at this point I started to make more 'computer art' than 'computer games'.

I do think that we artists need to be very suspicious of the habits of style, method and technique conveyed by the tools we use - something that extends to truly independent game development. Every tool engenders unique use patterns and aesthetic expectations, a reason to be be wary of 'standardising' on software and operating systems like those of Adobe, Apple, Discreet, Idsoftware and so forth. We need to remember that these ways of working are not uncontestable givens, just particular ways of working with a computer designed and implemented with a mass market in mind. 'Think Similar (TM)'.

I believe it's significantly more fruitful to celebrate the unusual, complex unexpected in software and have higher expectations than merely 'intuitive' tools and 'sexy' interfaces. Would the greats of painting have accepted such restrictions or the persistent presence of a Microsoft or Apple logo in their studios? I don't want that. Computers are a raw tool for me and I bend them to my needs, right down to the look and feel.

Free and Open Source software provide a great platform for independent development, even if only to shake the creator out of their 'industry standardised' assumptions. Hacking and modification are a great start, but just the beginning of a truly rigorous practice!

You also work as teacher. If you compare your own research and teaching practices with your current students, how is the notion of Game Art perceived?

- I think the expectations of students are both greater and smaller than they were 10 years ago: students now seem to want to get back to gaming's roots (like making 2d platformers for a mobile phone) or creating complex projects like augmented-reality, socially-networked MMOs. As what people consider a 'computer game' has significantly diversified over the last decade, so have students' interests and expectations.

Can you tell me some about your latest work "New Arena Painting"?
- This project ultimately began in 2003 with me experimenting developing visuals for my experimental music performances. While experimenting with the Quake III renderer I saw what looked to me like the beginning of a platform for generating rich, abstract expressionist paintings. So, 'q3aPaint' was born.

Since then I've refined it significantly, the most recent result of which is The New Arena Paintings, recently appearing at a solo show in Dundee, Scotland, as high-quality, large format prints. This new system is built atop the free and open source implementation of QuakeIII, 'IOQuake3'.

The interview took place in April 2010.

Joseph Delappe: "Howl" (2001)

Joseph DeLappe is a 2008 Commissioned Resident Artist at the Eyebeam Art and Technology Center in New York City. He is an Associate Professor of the Department of Art at the University of Nevada where he runs the Digital Media area. Working with electronic and new media since 1983, his work in online gaming performance, electromechanical installation and real time web-based video transmission have been shown throughout the United States and abroad.

You were among the first Game Artists to perform online. Why did you choose this format? What games did you use and why?
-The first works I created that involved computer games were in 1998-99. I created an appendage to my computer mouse that allowed for the attachment of a pencil and later brushes - "The Artist's Mouse" was invented as a way of reverse engineering this ubiquitous interface device. Probably two-three years prior to this I had first started to serious play computer games - as I recall one of the first was free game that came with my apple laptop - I think it was a version of "Battlezone" (I had briefly played this game and a Starwars game on arcade systems in the early 1980's). After "Battlezone" I played through Bungie's "Marathon" series, games that came for free with equipment that was ordered for my lab at the university where I teach. There were other games, "X-wing" and such that were played along the way. The invention of "The Artist's Mouse" created a situation where I logically moved towards using this device while playing a computer game as the mouse action was rather intense during game play. As such, the first game engaged in this manner just happened to be what I was playing at the time, the first iteration of "Unreal". I replaced my mouse pad with 10x10" sheets of fine arts rag paper and proceeded to play using the mouse with pencil attached. The results were quite pleasing and unexpected - abstract drawings that literally mapped the experience of going through several levels of this very popular and violent FPS game.

Sometime thereafter games were released that utilized online gameplay. I think the first of this type that I tried was "Quake". I was immediately struck by the use of texting to communicate between players. Typing on a keyboard while immersed in a fully realized 3D graphic virtual gamespace on the face of it seemed wonderfully anachronistic. Anyway, to make a long story short - the texting is what stood out to me - in the end, similar to utilzing graphite pencils to map gaming experience (an intentionally anachronistic conceptual gesture), engaging in text based performance in online game spaces soon emerged as an idea. It was in the spring of 2001 that I engaged in my first online gaming performance - "Howl: Elite Force Voyager Online". I entered the game as Allen Ginsberg and proceeded to perform the entirety of his seminal beat poem "Howl", word for word. I had no idea whether this was interesting or important or innovative. I was not aware of any other artists at that time engaged in using FPS games for artistic purposes - I very may well be the first to engage this particular genre for performative actions - although artists such as Anne-Marie Schleiner and Eddo Stern were engaged in game based projects around the same time frame. I am not so sure about the timelines here, might be worth looking into, but for sure I was unaware of any other artists at the time working with chat performances in shooter games. I did later learn of a wonderful project to perform "Waiting for Godot" that took place in a chatroom well prior to my work.

There is a long tradition in performance art to stretch the boundaries of what it is commonly understood as "art". The same trait is clearly visible in your own work. Which performance artist do you admire most, and perhaps, had the biggest impact on you?
-Most definitely. Linda Montano visited my university while I was in graduate school. Her work in bring art into life as performance - spending a year living with everything being the same color, being tied to the artist Sam Hseih for a year, etc - these works I found very inspiring. As well Laurie Anderson's early NYC street based performance "Duets on Ice". Oddly, it has been primarily women performance artists who I find most interesting - excluded from the galleries and museums they took to the streets and to life to make

their creative statements. I first engaged in performing in game spaces upon the realization that these online environments could be considered a new type of public space. I definitely consider my work to have a direct lineage to street theater/interventions, etc.

What should artist look for in online spaces? Is there something inherently challenging about online performances, compared to, let's say, real-life performances?
- The internet presents artists a new territory for creative engagement. Online games and communities are attractive to me as an artist for any number of reasons. There is definitely an intentional interest in reaching an audience outside of the artworld while at the same time being keenly aware of my context as a contemporary artist practicing in a complex history of interventionist performance art. I am also an artist living in an area that is possibly about as remote from the artworld as you might imagine - living in the high-desert of Nevada the internet and gaming in specific has presented me with a venue for creative exploration that allows my isolation as an artist to be negated. The potential for reaching a global audience is very seductive - although I must say that upon starting these works with "Howl" I had no sense that I was engaging in works that would eventually reach said audience in a very big way. Another motivation is that I have been working in computer media since 1983 - I recall vividly my first experience of artists working with the internet, likely in 1989, while at the same time coming of age as an artist during an era where "virtual reality" was the topic de riguer. I have always been skeptical of the utopian underpinnings of the art, science and technology community. Something that most attracted me to computer games, shooters in particular, was for me that these games somehow represent the popular realization of the over hyped promise of virtual reality. That is, it is very curious that we can create amazing 3D simulated environments for internet based interactions yet these interactions seem so primarily focused on killing each other over and over again. As well, it is a subversive stance to say that online gaming environments represent a new type of public space. I am an artist very concerned with reaching an audience - with

affecting change - one cannot do so working in a vacuum (whether that vaccuum is the private artist's studio or the art world). Very important to me that the work get out there in a way that both represents taking agency and presenting creative experiences that interrupt or intervene within these online contexts.

How did the audience react to your performances? And how about the critics? Back then there were not that many artists subverting the dynamics on online games.
-I think it was in 2000 when I was invited to show documentation of the "Howl: Elite Force Voyager Online" performance at the Art Fair in Santa Fe, New Mexico. I was invited by Refusalon of San Francisco to actually re-perform this work but discovered that the convention hall lacked internet access. As such, we played a looping document of the reading of "Howl" with the game - at times at quite a loud volume. This was quite fun and actually garnered quite a bit of attention from the visitors to this event. I do not recall any criticism being written specifically about this showing. My work in computer games really took off after the publication of an article by Matt Mirapaul of the New York Times regarding the "Quake/Friends" performance in 2003. I was threatened with legal action by Warner Brothers TV and quite excited by the exposure.

Your performances breas the players' illusion of what is commonly called "the magic circle", the idea that game-spaces are somehow sacred and separated from "real life". You deliberately break this fantasy, making the players aware of the reality that lies outside the simulation, a kind of Brechtian Verfrumdungseffekt. How do players react to your interventions?
- I see these works as a way to break through and perhaps expand the notion of "the magic circle" in gaming. We do not "play" in contexts that are unrelated to our political, social and economic realities. Reactions during the first performance, "Howl" were mostly humorous. I recall one player noting "wow, poetry and shooting!" Reactions to my work have been most fierce within the context of the ongoing project, "dead-in-iraq", commenced in 2006. Other players routinely insult me, demand to know why I am doing

what I am doing and are generally very hostile. There have, however, been instances of other players defending my actions, saying things like "what is wrong with what he is doing?" I even know of two players who at one point decided to stand in front of my avatar and take bullets so that I could continue my reading. What has been very interesting and unexpected has been engaging in debates on the internet outside of the game proper. These have evolved with the publication of numerous online and print articles about the work - upon reading some of the comments from the readers I decided to join the ensuing debates. These have proven very interesting and, as I see them, they represent a unique opportunity for me to engage in dialogue with those either experiencing the work first hand or interested in commenting upon the project, whether pro or con.

I am really fascinated by "War Poetry: Medal of Honor, Allied Assault Online", a performance in which you read Sigfried Sassoon's poetry during a session of Medal of Honor. Why did you choose this artist and this game?
-Siegfried Sassoon and Wilfred Owen are two famous British soldiers who, during World War 1 wrote amazing poetry regarding their experiences in the trenches. Both of them were sent to a mental institution (where they met) due to their resistance to the war. Their poetry is amazing, moving and timeless. The notion of reciting their poetry was a specific reaction to the start of the War in Iraq in 2003. This was my first step in computer games into works that I would consider anti-war activism in computer games. The other works, "Howl", "Quake/Friends" and such have perhaps more of an ironic stance that indeed create critical contexts for the consideration of culture - they are a bit more fun. With the "War Poetry" project my work began to take on a more serious tone, again, reflecting the drumbeat to war - most definitely this work should be considered a precursor to the "dead-in-iraq" intervention.

The interview took place in May 2010.

Stephen Honegger: "Container" (2002)

Born in South Africa in 1974, Stephen Honegger was among the first Australian artists to experiment with videogames and achieve worldwide recognition. His first major work is the video installation "Container" developed with Anthony Hunt in 2002 and exhibited at the Gertrude Contemporary Art Space in Melbourne, Australia. Container, is based around the format of a video game. Set inside a full-scale replica of a shipping container, gallery visitors can experience the unsettling feeling of being hunted as they view a projected video, created with 3D modelling software, depicting a sinister event filmed within the gallery space. He also worked on "Escape from Woomera" (2003), a modification of Half-Life that challenged the Australian immigration policy.

One of your seminal works, "Container" (2002) is an extremely original and powerful combination of interactive art and gaming aesthetics. What were your goals and what kinds of tools did you use to create the videogame sequence?

- Container came about as a solution to the problem of creating a dark enough space in the gallery to project a video. Our solution was to build an enclosed space within the gallery but had no idea what that structure would be and how it would tie in with the content of a video. At the time, I was building a Counter-Strike map of a shipping container yard, so we decided to make a scale replica of a shipping container to project the video inside. We came up with the idea of creating a narrative, using the Half-Life engine, describing how this improbable object may have manifested itself in the gallery. I used a modified version of the Half-Life engine called Spirit of Half-Life to build everything in the video sequence. A few years later Container was remade for shows in Sydney and Korea.

Was "Container" your first Game Art project?

- I first started using games in my art work in 1998. I made a video called 'More Dance' which was a recording of characters from the Playstation game Tekken. In their idle animation loops with a pounding electro sound track, it looked like the characters were dancing with each other instead of getting ready to fight.

You also developed another milestone in the history of Game Art and the "Serious Games" movement, "Escape from Woomera" (2003). What role did you play in the development of "Escape from Woomera" and how you got involved?
-I was lead environment artist on "Escape from Woomera" and responsible for modelling and texturing the Woomera detention centre. My friend, Julian Oliver put my name forward to the creator of the game because he knew that I had experience using the Half-Life engine and that I was concerned about the plight of refugees in Australia's refugee detention system.

Was "Escape from Woomera" well received by the public?
- The game achieved its goal a long time before it was even released. The title of the game and the fact that it was funded by the Australian government was enough to be controversial and get people talking before anyone actually played the game. By the time that it was released to the public in 2004, the Woomera detention centre had already been shut down. I like to think that Escape from Woomera played a small part in the detention centres demise and drew attention to the plight of refugees.

Australia has always been at the forefront of innovation, when it comes to Game Art and game-based artistic interventions. Why is that?
-When I first started making artwork using games, I had no idea that there were other people doing the same thing in Australia. Only after meeting Julian Oliver and Chad Chatterton did I realise that artist were using games across an array of artistic disciplines. Julian was doing amazing things with interactive environments and audio design and Chad, like myself had just started to explore the possibilities of creating environments with a game engine. Those two guys where the catalyst for myself and many other artists in Melbourne to realise the potential of using game engines as part of their art practice.

People working in the Australian game development industry also turned to making game art and independent games such as Escape from Woomera. They felt that they were unable to have much creative input into the commercial games that they were developing and wanted to make games which they had more control over and had more meaningful content.

You're both creating artistic project with videogames and developing artworks for commercial games. How do you see these two contexts? Are they in opposition or are they somehow communicating with each other?

- I really enjoy working as a game artist, it's a lot of fun making interesting landscapes and objects for games. I have been pretty lucky though, and have generally worked on projects that I am interested in. Obviously there are constraints and limitations placed on you creatively when working for a commercial developer. Making art for a gallery space is a kind of privilege, a unique opportunity to do something new. As a contemporary artist, you are not constrained by the limitations of any one medium and you are able to create an experience for the viewer that cannot be done anywhere else. That is the biggest attraction for me in making artwork for a gallery space, not limiting myself to any one medium and trying to create something new and original.

I think that commercial video games are not paid the same artistic dues as other art forms such as film and literature because of the term 'game'. Games are generally considered somewhat trivial. To be honest though, I don't really want games to be aligned with other accepted forms of art. I like the way that games have created a new realm that doesn't sit very comfortably with other existing art forms.

The interview took place in June 2010.

Eddo Stern: "Vietnam Romance" (2003)

Eddo Stern works on the disputed borderlands between fantasy and reality, exploring the uneasy and otherwise unconscious connections between physical existence and electronic simulation. His work explores new modes of narrative and documentary, experimental computer game design, fantasies of technology and history, and cross-cultural representation in computer games, film, and online media. He works in various media including computer software, hardware and game design, kinetic sculpture, performance, and film and video production. His short machinima films include "Sheik Attack", "Vietnam Romance", "Landlord Vigilante" and "Deathstar". He is the founder of the now retired cooperative C-level where he co-produced the physical computer gaming projects "Waco Resurrection", "Tekken Torture Tournament", "Cockfight Arena", and the internet meme conference "C-level Memefest"

What is your relationship to videogames?
- I started playing and making computer games on an Apple II+ in the early 1980s. I was a member of the Be'er Sheva computer club, cracking games and doublesiding floppies with a round hole punch till someone built a square floppy disk nibbler. Some of my more memorable game playing experiences were with Autoduel, Timezone, Castle Wolfenstein, Aztec, Ruski Duck, Utlima, Zork, Drol, and Karateka. I've been interested in and studied math, philosophy and then art. In trying to combine all three, games eventually became the solution, a new "gesamtkunstwerk". My earliest art work was installation focused. After that I worked with pretty high end VR for a few years - but VR seemed so stale compared to gaming culture, and I really like low tech tinkerering. I am very interested in total immersion but not in a strictly visual or haptic way - and I think my approach to gaming reflects this.

You were a member of the now legendary collective C-level? How did it start?
-C-Level was both a group or people and an artist run space. I started with a few friends right after graduate school. The initial

idea behind C-level was to create a space and working environment outside of school that mirrored the Integrated Media Lab at CalArts which most of us had shared. C-level was supposed to be a workspace that broke from the tradition of the segregated artist studio. In the beginning C-level was just that - a space where we worked and shared equipment, an artist co-op. Eventually things shifted and C-level became a public space which produced and hosted events, and soon after become more well known as gaming lab and often miscatagorized as an "artist group" as a few of the gaming projects become well known (Tekken Torture Tournament, Cockfigtht Arena and Waco Resurrection), but there was plenty going on at C-level that had nothing to do with gaming.

"Waco Resurrection" is one of the most celebrated works by C-level. Why creating a game about the Waco incident?
- The idea for the Waco game came into existence as an amalgam of forces and arbitrary events (as does anything? perhaps...). I had been interested in the intersection of real events/history with gaming, and had been exploring this using video (Machinima) specifically with works like Rock Attack, Sheik Attack and Vietnam Romance. Michael Wilson (from C-level), was working on a sound piece about Waco at the time, and this helped spark our interest in researching the specifics of the Branch Dividians. The connections between religious beliefs, constructed mythologies and historical fantasy (super powers and a self published religious text) were starting points for exploring the Waco events as a "subjective" documentary rather than an accurate historical reenactment through game. In addition to this, me, Mark Allen and Jessica Hutchins had just finished the Tekken and Cockfight physical game performances and were ready for a more ambitious game project that also involved a physical (off-screen component). We then recruited Peter Brinson and Brody Condon to join the team and started working on Waco Resurrection - three month later we were done. One of the differences in making a game about an historical event is the nature of identification and implication. Game require the users to act and such appear to implicate the player in the actions of the avatar they are controlling. This is rather obvious but

does create new emotional experiences. Imagine a documentary about Hitler vs. a fictional film with an actor playing as Hitler vs. a game where the player plays as Hitler. The most common criticisms we heard about Waco were that the game is in bad taste, that the game is exploitative, that the game was pro Dividian / pro Koresh. The bad taste and exploitation criticism stem from people struggling to consider that games can be made about serious issues while still providing some ambiguity. The second criticism of the game being politically skewed assumes that Koresh as a protagonist = a Hero in the game - a unique issue that games reveal as film about Hitler would likely not draw this criticism or a film about David Koresh.

You were among the first artists to experiment with machinima. Think for instance of Sheik Attack (1999) and Vietnam Romance (2003). Why were so fascinated by this format (medium?)? How did you create Sheik Attack?
-I made my first "machinima" in 1995 of my girlfriend playing Tetris with a voice over - recorded on high 8 off the screen. I later made "Rock Attack" recording a rehearsed scene in Command and Conquer using a VGA to TV converter, in 1996 and I thought I had invented something completely new until I was shown Miltos Manetas' "Flames" project recordings of Lara Croft dying on a PS1. "Sheik Attack" was a more ambitious project which took about 6 months to finish. Initially I created a storyboard and then went looking for games that may provide footage to match my storyline, I then played the games over and over recording the screen trying to match the shots that I needed but with some improvisational moments, I think I have about 10 hours of footage for the 16 minute final video. Only midway through this process did I recognize the extra-textual connection between the games' titles and release dates and their correspondence to the events in Lebanon that I was trying to recreate. For "Vietnam Romance" I had a mix of very precise film scenes that I tried to recreate frame by frame in games and this was a pretty challenging process from a game play standpoint. Trying to match the helicopter landing scene from the TV show M.A.S.H. took a few whole days of game play. Also trying to find the right deer to shoot in the right way to match "The Deer

Hunter" was not so easy and I will adamant to resorting to cheat codes to spawn the damn animal at the right place - even that took about a day :)

Do you see any difference working with machinima and a more traditional style of video art?
- I think it depends on the context of the video and what you are trying to say or do. Many Machinima works are self referential - in the sense that they exist in the same cultural context as the game(s) they are using. My choice of specific games for my Machinima are determined by something else I want to say. My subject matter is not much concerned with self references to game culture (you'll notice that most Machinima is comic in nature) as it is to a wider cultural context for the intersection of history, violence and simulation. So to answer your question I do think that presenting work as Machinima assumes a context of game culture (and a more mainstream / lighthearted expectation from the work). Whereas presenting the same work as videoart in a museum / gallery brings a noter set of expectations and another set of viewers, likely not familiar with the game culture context and likely used to a shorter non-linear viewing experience. Showing the same work in a film festival brings with it yet a noter set of expectations and viewing practices. For my Machinima films I find that film festivals have often offered the best viewing context - not unexpectedly in terms of migrating the visual experience away from the computer screen which is something that is important to me when showing my Machinima. I was inspired to make video by a piece called "Dial H-I-S-T-O-R-Y" by Johan Grimonprez. Unlike many works of video art which document a performance or offer footage of repetitive goings-on, Dial was an intensely entrancing immersive experience, and yet did not rely on conventional narrative to achieve its immersiveness.

As an artist experimenting with videogames, what is your relationship with the art market?
- My work exists in various art/economic contexts. Some of my works are free, some are editioned, some are one of a kind objects,

some are distributed, some are self published, some are sold, bought and shown by galleries and Museums.

The interview took place in June 2010.

Axel Stockburger: "Tokyo Arcade Warriors" (2003)

Born in 1974, "Axel Stockburger is an artist and theorist who lives and works in London and Vienna. He studied at the University of Applied Arts in Vienna with Peter Weibel and holds a PhD from the University of the Arts, London. His films and installations are shown internationally. Among other projects he has initiated the independent art television channel TIV in Vienna in 1998 and collaborated on international projects with the London based media art group D-Fuse (2000-2004). At present he works as scientific staff member at the Department for Visual Arts and Digital Media/Academy of Fine Arts in Vienna." (from artist's bio)

What is your relationship with videogames? When did you start playing? What games did you like?

- My first contact with videogames must have been visiting game arcades during holidays in Italy as a child. The games I loved ranged from Wonderboy over Pac-Man and the various renditions of Space Invaders. A little bit later a schoolfriend got a Commodore 64, which became a center of attention for a period of time. I will always remember the chuckling sound the little goblin in Barbarians made when it kicked the pixellated severed head of the opponents that would be left lying on the ground into a hole. After this period my gaming became infrequent and i remember playing adventure games like the Monkey Island series, Day of the Tentacle and Indiana Jones on the PC. Between 14 and 18 I lost track of gaming and my interest awoke again when i started to study media arts at the University for Applied Arts in Vienna under Professor Peter Weibel, who at the time was producing and curating interactive art pieces. We went to see works at the Ars Electronica in Linz, among them the works of artists like Jeffrey Shaw, which were usually produced with expensive Silicon Graphics Computers.

At the same time however, the students started to play Doom at night in the studios on cheap PC's. The idea to play against other human beings inside a simulated space really fascinated me and I was convinced that while we were being thaught about the fine art side of things there was a popular mass media universe that had already taken a whole step further into an exciting direction. I became hooked with online FPS games when Quake emerged on the scene. I clearly remember one night at the studio when i was still a relative newbie. I was there alone, waiting for some render jobs for a video piece, when I decided to play a round of Quake. In the first two hours I was regularly blasted to pieces and I didn't fully understand where the people were finding all the extra weapons and gear that I never seemd to be able to get. I became a bit frustrated and hopped between servers a lot, when I ended up on a Canadian server, playing against a single opponent who was clearly much more skilled and knowledgeable than me. After fragging me about 30 times we started to chat, and he decided to introduce me to the game space by leading me through the different levels, showing me all the secret paths, locations of items and hidden bits and pieces. We spent a good part of a night in 1996 doing this, and I will never forget the experience. On my way home in the morning I began to think about what had just happened and I realised that this was something entirely new for me: to share a spatial, performative experience with somebody as far away as Canada.

At this point I have to admit that I never became particularly good at any video or computer game. In this sense I don't consider myself a gamer. Quite often I actually enjoyed it more to watch other people play so I would be able to see what comes next without having to putt he effort in. The explorative side of gaming combined with moments of emergence and the potential to affect the action (even if this just means to co-pilote somebody else through a tricky sequence of a game) was what interested me at the time. Up to this day I often enjoy not to have to do too much in a game. To give you an example I remember using GTA as a kind of video synthesizer in the sense that I enjoyed to jump onto the roof of a car and just let it drive through the city, thereby generating chance encounters and situations that were aesthetically pleasing to me. I guess this slightly passive involvement in gaming led me to watch other people who were playing much more closely and I began to wonder why I was so captured by this image. If you didn't watch the screen, but the people themselves, they seemed to be immersed in a different kind of reality, completely shutting out the rest of their environment. To me this image became a very strong metaphor for our entanglement with technology, an image that captures with the utmost precision what millions of humans are engaged in every day when they interact with symbolic machines.

You wrote and defended your thesis, "THE RENDERED ARENA Modalities of Space in Video and Computer Games, in 2006. When did you make a conscious decision about investigating videogames academically? Why? There were not that many researchers interested in this topic, back then...
- What led me to do research into games was my fascination with the medium that had emerged from my artistic work. My art is guided by a thorough interest in mediated spatiality, ranging from film over sound to digital games. In a number of videopieces I wanted to capture the odd situation of people simultaneously engaged with the physical world and mediated space. Since fine art and especially painting has long been concerned with the creation of spatial representation I realised that by focusing on these aspects in the context of digital games I might be able to find out how the practices of generating such representations are changing and bringing about novel forms of art. When I started my research I was puzzled that issues of spatiality did not seem to interest many scholars in the field of game studies. The focus was on narrative and ludic structures in games and a more complex conceptualisation of the aspects of spatiality did not seem to exist. I started my PhD as a practice based research project funded by the London University of the Arts.

Thus I had a lot of freedom to develop a very subjective research agenda. At first I asked myself how one could conceptualise the role of sound for spatial representation in digital games. This question emerged from a series of experiments I had made with video/sound installations that concentrated on "acousmatic" situations, which were meant to create specific kinds of spaces inbetween sound and vision. I had read Michel Chion's work about sound in films, which had influenced my video pieces and I thought that a similar analysis was missing in the field of games. Since then there has been a lot of excellent work in this direction, but at the time this issue seemed to have been neglected to a certain degree. Then I began to ask myself how I could possibly talk about space and spatiality, which is obviously an immensily important subject throughout the history of Philosophy, without considering the history of thinking about space and I spent nearly three years reading about space in contexts reaching from Physics, Fine Art and Architecture over to the Humanities.

Finally I settled for Henri Lefebvre's concept of space as a social product that is informed by aspects of the conceptual and the lived. Based on this concept it was possible to develop a modelt hat aims to explain how the different elements that are dynamically interconnected with each other when it comes to the kind of spatiality generated by computer games can be understood as unique elements working together as a system. I wanted to demonstrate that this spatiality is the result of a dense web of distinctive practices and elements, ranging from the narrative (for example tales of journey and exploration) over images and sounds, rules as well as the physical involvement of the players. It was a very interesting task for me to map out a kind of model that would be able to explain how this different kind of spatiality is created, but also how it is related to historical forms and devices. At the same time I started to research artistic approaches to game spaces and made an effort to show how these, often experimental pieces, were dealing with some of questions and issues that had appeared throughout my other inquiries.

As a researcher and a practitioner, how would you describe the evolution of Game Art? Can you name a few milestones? An influential work or artist that left a mark in the history of Game Art?

- At first I have to state that the I have a very sceptical stance towards the term "game art" because I am convinced that the creation of such niches does not do the works justice. Just as the term "video art" has lost it's purpose because the medium has become an essential part of so many different artistic endevours in contemporary art that it simply has become obsolete, game art should not become a term that limits the possibilities of artists and artworks to cross the boundaries established by economic realities and academic categorisation. I think it is necessary to maintain a broader perspective and realise that some of the works that are currently being tagged as "game art" belong to a much longer tradition, since games and play have been important paradigms throughout the history of modern art. In this sense I would start with the unique language games and the general importance of play in the work of Marcel Duchamp and bring up the Situationist approach to the notion of play.

I am convinced that games can be regarded as models for different social practices and issues. They allow a specific sharpening of the focus because they are capable of generating temporary worlds. Personally I really like the work of the Israeli artist Uri Tzaig. For me the piece "Universal Square" (1997) is a seminal work, because it shows how a tiny change of the rules of a game can have a huge ripple effect. This work is about the football game between an Israeli team against a Palestinian team and Tzaig simpl introduces a second ball. It is at once a perfect metaphor pointing towards the political reality of the Israeli Palestinian conflict but it also works on a very subtle level in relation to media systems, for example when the TV teams that were present to transmit the event became increasingly confused where to point their cameras. Another great example for work that does not rely on computers is the art of Gabriel Orozco, who has introduced toys, games and playing fields in his work as a means to enrich his philosophical inquiries. In relation to artistic work based on computer and video games i am much less interested in approaches that deal with the ever shifting aesthetics found in games, but mainly those that manage to embedd their work in a wider context of art and philosophy and adopt a conceptual approach. For example, Joseph DeLappe's works are very important from my point of view because they try to point their finger at the emergence of new types of audiences for artistic interventions. There are few artists that manage to adopt the aesthetical potential of computer games and introduce concepts that take the medium beyond.

The works of Sylvia Eckermann and Mathias Fuchs was very important in that respect because they initially conceived 3D games as vehicles for knowledge production and dissemination. At present there are too many interesting artists whose work is influenced by game paradigms to name. In general I have to say that I am convinced that the transformations brought about by contemporary game culture, ranging from the formation of new forms of cooperation and collaborative engagement to the ability of interconnecting and contextualising a myriad of different cultural forms will deeply affect how we produce and consume what has been called art up to this point. The convergence between different narrative strategies, technologies and media systems will only become productive as a backdrop for novel and unique works of art if we manage to look beyond the confines of specific territories, such as the entertainment industry, the academic sphere or the art market.

As an artist, you have been documenting the gamer scene since 1996, as beautifully illustrated by such works as "Tokyo Arcade Warriors", a series of videos that portrait players of video and computer games shot in a public game arcade in Shinjuku/Tokyo,"Boys in the Hood", "PSX Warriors: Gran Turismo", and "Head Mounted Display". Can you tell me what are so interesting with gamers and how it all started? Is there any kind of gamers that you are particularly interested in?
- In 1997 i made a video piece called "Head Mounted Display", were i projected the imagery of a network game called spectre supreme onto the mirrored sunglasses of a person that did not move at all. The only movement was the game action, refracted through the mirror lenses of his shades. This piece was influenced by a lot SF writers like William Gibson and his notion of cyber space but also by writings of Jean Baudrillard about simulation. I wanted to create an ironical commentary about the expensive interactive art pieces that were shown in museums at the time by using a cheap mass media game. At the same time technological developments like the so called Head Mounted Displays developed by military research fascinated me.

In a philosophical sense I wanted to make a point about the platonic tradition of idealism and it's relation to contemporary media. The images projected onto the sunglasses were platonic shapes, ideal forms that were reflected from the body of the observer who was to remain in shackles. This singular "player", did not move at all and was merely a means for projection. Later I began to observe players and their body movements more closely ("PSX Warriors – Tekken"). I became fascinated by the remnants and traces of body movements by players playing fighting or racing games. They did not need to tilt their bodies in the direction of their vehicles at every curve but somehow their bodies involuntarily shadowed the virtual spaces they were moving in.

Around this time in the late 90s there was a debate about bodies being lost in cyberspace examplified by the writings of Baudrillard about the fractal subject. However, as I observed these bodies were very present and their gestures during gameplay made that obvious. With the introduction of motion sensors and systems like the WII the importance of bodies in front of the screen has been adressed and the situation is slightly different today. A second strain of inquiry in my artistic work was opened when I started to record interviews by people who had played games like GTA 3 ("Boys in the Hood"). Here I was interested in the tiny difference between real action and actions performed in a game environment. The accounts of the players who were talking about their in game actions appeared so "real" because they had „really" done what they were talking about. The feeling of unease that emerges when a young men tells you with the greatest sincerity that he has just shot a few gang members in order to get a new car was interesting for me.

Additionally these interview pieces addressed audiences in different ways. People who knew the game became interested because they could relate to the places and actions the players were talking about, while those who were ignorant of such games were simultaneously fascinated and disgusted by the stories (starting to imagine the wildest things). Overall, these interviews dealt with the question how the experience of a 3D game environment triggers our memories of spaces and events. I had a very interesting experience in Moscow a few years ago, when I walked across the red square, where I had never physically been, and I knew exactly were to expect buildings and entrances because I had played a First Person Shooter with maps based on its architectural layout. I thought that this was a unique experience that was connected to the novel spatiality of the medium and I wanted to work about this.

In my recent works related to games ("Goldfarmer") I started to research the economics of games like World of Warcraft because I realised that phenomena like the outsourcing of gold farming (players playing for money) from Europe to Asia, were an interesting small scale model of global economical developments. This is why I decided to interview one of the first gold farmers in Europe who came from Denmark, in order to hear how this micro economy started. Since this person wanted to remain anonymous I decided after the interview to track his head motion and put the head of his in game Avatar (an Ork) over his face.

This piece asks what it means when the borders between play for enjoyment and relaxation changes place with the toil of work and how the borders between work and play are redrawn and at times erased by contemporary economic developments. My latest works ("Bestiarium", "Spellbound") have shifted from direct references to digital games towards phenomena of global narratives and franchises like harry potter and pokemon. I want to trace how and why the interest in these narratives is shared by a global community of fans and which kind of specific knowledge is created around these phenomena. At present I am part of a research project where i am working in this direction.

As an artist and academic researcher, do you recognize an intellectual or cultural gap between the art world and the academic world when it comes to artistic practices based on game aesthetics and game technology?

-From my point of view it is impossible to generalize how games and play have been regarded in the art world or the academic environment. It seems that wether they are taken seriously as cultural and artistic forms depends to a large extent on the personal experiences of artists and researchers. At times it seems that more traditional parts of the art establishment have certain problems with guarding the cultural border between high brow intellectual endevours and that which is perceived as cheap entertainment media. However, many examples show that this changes with the diversification of games and the fact that an increasing number of people is exposed to them. We have seen this hostility towards new forms of media and expression a lot of times before, if we consider for example the relationship between Pop Art and Comics, or the integration of popular culture in the form of music or fashion into the context of fine art.

I am however convinced that the cultural transformation brought about by the Internet and digital culture already has a much stronger impact on the bourgeois traditions of elitist fine art circles than most people realise. The emergence of cultural islands which form themselves around specific contents and interests will affect traditional separations between cultural fields and bring about changes that can be witnessed in their economical, social and political restructuring. The impact of new forms of participatory culture increasingly changes the way we perceive art and science. Early signs of this change can already be seen in the growing interest for game culture in art and academia, because this field enables people from a wide range of disciplines to observe and understand new forms of meaningful global interaction. The gap between the engagement in online game universes and "real world" political grassroots action is closing fast.

The interview took place in June 2010.

Andy Clarke and Grethe Mitchell: Game Art Criticism

In 2006, Andy Clarke and Grethe Mitchell edited the book "Videogames and Art" (UP Chicago, 2006). The antologhy was one of the first academic books about video games and art.

When did your interest for videogames begin, and what prompted you to investigate the relationship between art and games?
- We were interested in videogame studies before there were videogame studies conferences to present at. We started off writing about videogames in relation to film, looking at the way in which different camera viewpoints affect the user's level of involvement. That was for the "Visual Narrative Matrix" conference in 1999. We both have a film degree followed by one in interactive design, so it was natural to combine the theoretical approaches of the two
We got interested in videogame art in particular because we were more interested in looking at activities towards the edge of videogame studies, rather than at the mainstream. We were already interested in other forms of digital art like net.art and dance technology, so videogame art was on our radar very early on. We could tell straight away that it was going to be significant – the work was just so interesting and varied, both in terms of its techniques and ideas it was exploring.

What was the background and goals of the COSIGN conference? Back in the early Zeros, "game studies" as an academic discipline was relatively new... What was the reaction of the Ivory Tower to the emergence of this eclectic field? How have Game Studies evolved in the past decade?
- COSIGN was a great series of conferences and something that we are both very proud of. We were doing something unique for the time – bringing together artists, theorists and computer scientists – and managed to create a really special atmosphere that has left a lasting impression on those who attended.

COSIGN came about because we saw a gap. There were lots of different people looking, in different ways, at meaning: how we create meaning with computers, how we get computers to understand meaning, how we understand the meaning of things created with computers. We just brought them all together. We were one of the first conferences to bring together artists and computer scientists.

There were two things that we did which were crucial to the unique atmosphere. The first was that everyone got treated equally. The computer scientists and the artists all got the same time to present and the same space in the proceedings. The second was that there were no streams. That meant everyone got exposed to everything. And we didn't even restrict it to digital artists – it could be painters and sculptors as well. So on the first day of the first conference, we had a paper from MIT followed by one from an artist from Brazil who did interactive poetry.

When COSIGN started, there weren't any of the big videogame conferences like we have now. There were some conferences and people writing papers here and there, but no focus to the community. We attracted a broad range of videogame-related papers because of that.

How would you describe the genesis of Game Art? When and why did artists begin to use videogames in their artistic interventions? Who were the pioneers?

-One of the things that we tried to get across in our book was that videogame art didn't start in 1999 with "Cracking the Maze". There were artists working with videogames before that – it is just that they weren't calling themselves videogame artists (because that wasn't a term). They also weren't being put together in exhibitions of videogame art because there weren't any.

We think that Suzanne Treister's fake game boxes and fake videogame stills from 1991/92 are a really groundbreaking work and would regard her as one of the first videogame artists. There are probably people before that, but it becomes difficult to separate their activity from the demo scene, game hacking, etc. With Treister, it is clear that this is art: you have someone who is established as an artist, and getting it shown at a commercial gallery.

If you had to pick your favourite Game Art piece from the "early years", what would that be?
-It is very hard to single out one work, but if we define the "early years" as pre-2001 (and exclude Treister who we have already mentioned), then I think we would have to say "Adam KIller". When people think about videogame art, they think about that one and fifty years from now, when videogame art is mainstream, people will still be looking at that as an example. "Adam Killer" is an artwork that is clearly made with a videogame, deals with videogames as its subject matter, and doesn't try to replicate reality. Other ones that come to mind are Jon Haddock's "Isometric Screenshots" series and the work of Beige.

Let's talk about "Videogame and Art", a milestone in Game Art criticism. When did you come up with the idea to create a book? Did you have any trouble finding contributors and/or a publisher for a project dedicated to a relatively new and rather niche - at least back then - artform? How was the book received?
- We felt, at that time, that there was a videogame art movement that was beginning to gain momentum, but we could also feel that it was changing – some of the artists would crossover into the mainstream, the games would change and become either easier or harder to work with, people would move on to new ideas or techniques.
So we had three aims with the book. Firstly, we wanted to document this "magic" period and some of the major artists. We felt it was important to do this at the time, rather than retrospectively. Secondly, we wanted to cover a broad range and highlight some less well-known artists and activities like in-game performance which weren't getting as much exposure as the FPS mods. And finally, we wanted to sketch out some of the critical/theoretical framework within which this work fits.
We initially had a French publisher that we found as a result of a presentation that we gave on videogame art (and appropriation in

general) at "La Villette Numerique" (2002). On the basis of that, we put out the call and selected the articles for the book. But there were some problems and we had to find another publisher. That was quite stressful as people were already excited about the book – also our contributors had already put a lot of work into their essays, and we didn't want to disappoint them. A couple of people recommended Intellect Books and they were the first and only company we approached. They have been really good to us and we are very pleased with the end result.

With regard to finding the writers, we put out an open call for the book asking for essays. One of the things that we wanted to avoid was just "rounding up the usual suspects". That was a bit of a risk, but we thought it would be good to leave it to chance, as that would allow us to get a broader variety of topics and perspectives. in the end, it worked out extremely well.

You are also planning a sequel to "Videogames and Art", correct? How will it differ from the first installment? And how has Game Art changed since the publication of your book?

- The big change over recent years has been the increase in popularity. Videogame art is becoming more popular and more mainstream, as we expected. The tools have also become more sophisticated (particularly those for machinima).

Although we are still interested in the field and follow the artists in it, we didn't want to do a follow-up book which was just "Videogames and Art – The Next Generation" so we are planning an updated version of the book, rather than a sequel.

Our plan is to update some of the articles, particularly those that are on/by a single artist, to see how they have progressed since the book came out and to add some new articles, covering areas which have emerged as being more significant.

So, for instance, the work of Condon or De Lappe is now is different to the work they were doing then, and you want to know what has happened to Beyond Woomera since the book. Likewise, we had an article covering the early history of machinima, but this warrants more coverage now on the basis of how active that area has become.

There are also some emerging issues that we are exploring such as the relationship between videogame artists and commercial galleries. There is also the relationship between videogame companies and artists – which will become more of an issue as the price of videogame art increases.

The interview took place in July 2010.

Brody Condon: "Adam Killer" (1999)

"Brody Condon (born 1974, Mexico) is an American artist currently based in New York. Condon graduated with an MFA from the University of California San Diego, and attended residencies at the Skowhegan School of Painting and Sculpture and the Rijkakademie van Beeldende Kunsten in the Netherlands. His solo and collaborative work has been exhibited at the Whitney Biennial 2004, Pace Wildenstein Gallery and the New Museum of Contemporary Art in New York, the Santa Monica Museum of Art and Machine Project in Los Angeles, the Stedelijk Museum Amsterdam, and KW in Berlin. Concerned with the over-identification with fantasy in contemporary culture, Condon's work often finds its final form in performance, sculptural installation, and video. Following periods of historical and sociological research, the work often re-contextualizes and then modifies existing pop culture, historical events, as well as other artworks. Steeped in dark humour and a unsypathetic gaze into his own unreliable post traumatic memories, the work directly engages with various modes of "projection of self" into other spaces via computer and live roleplaying games, religious experience, psychoactive substances, and dissociative disorders."

How were videogames perceived by students and teachers while you were studying at University of California, San Diego? When did you begin to experiment with games? And why did you choose modding over other artistic practices?
- I began experimenting with game footage in videos during my undergrad. About '96 or '97. Nothing substantial came out of it. I learned all the skills/tools online from the mod subculture. In grad school professors like Lev Manovich offered their support, but a few professors actually refused to meet with me. They were simply not convinced I had anything to offer, they didn't understand the material. I showed the work publicly for a USCD undergrad class lecture, then at a graduate conference at UCLA. The first time someone started crying, everyone was yelling, and her friend accused me of inciting violence, so I threw a chair at the wall.

Everyone shut the fuck up, as it was immediately clear – the difference between images of violence and the actual thing. The second time someone yelled "bullshit" from the audience and I was told to stop presenting. The reaction to game imagery was different then, imagine... The Sims didn't even exist yet.

"Adam Killer" (1999) is a modification of Half-Life. What was your original intent with "Adam Killer"? Was that your first artistic intervention with games?
- I began modding Half-Life when I was living in a dirty hole in LA before grad school, I was not a happy human being. I started recreating the Columbine school where the shootings occurred. That's what I was doing when I came into UCSD. Thankfully I stopped that project and began making 3D portraits of friends and attempting to break the Half-Life engine, so Adam Killer was born about '99. I was thinking about the separation of media images from their actual context and meaning in my own life. I was thinking about minimalism, repetition, and psychedelic art. I wanted to re-connect somehow, make all of that time I wasted in front of the screen useful. So I shot the 3d character of my friend Adam (who always wore white) again and again and again. I could stand back and look at the carnage, at the bloody but painterly trails left by the glitched engine, and feel like all was right with the world. It was a performance, and the video documentation became the piece afterwards. I never released it as software.

You were a member of the group C-Level. Can you tell me how you got involved and what do you think was the most important work C-level created during its existence?
- I was never an official member of C-Level, that was Eddo Stern's thing. I was involved though, I considered them friends and they supported my work. My first public exhibition of the game work was simultaneously at C-Level and Miltos Manetas's space around the corner in Chinatown. I'm surprised Miltos showed the work, the first time he came into my studio he called me a loser. Thinking back I remember the first Tekken Torture Tournament as good times. We did eventually make Waco Resurrection together

however, and I think that may have been its most influential work. But I think its success began the breakup of the collective – but you would have to ask the C-Level members about that.

You were also a member of the Velvet-Strike team. Can you tell me how you did know the other members and what you remember from Whitney Biennal where "Velvet-Strike" was exhibited?

- I met Anne-Marie Schleiner when she came to UCSD as a visiting professor. She asked me, along with Joan Leandre from Barcelona who I hadn't met yet, to collaborate on a intervention within Counter-Strike. I think it was 2001 or 2002. Initially I felt it was overly didactic, but I trusted her instincts. The idea of games as internalized war propaganda had not been well articulated at that point. I am not sure if Anne-Marie or Joan cared so much about the Whitney Biennal. I came out of a traditional visual arts education, not media art, so it meant a lot to me. "Velvet Strike" was not a great piece for a exhibition like that, it was displayed poorly and I think its relevance was lost on most viewers. I seem to remember nice parties. I remember giving a lame lecture. Overall I was not ready for that sort of exposure.

In "Need for Speed" (Cargo Cult) you made a copy of a Lamborghini Countach extracted from the racing game Need for Speed. Why did you build a copy of a high-tech digital virtual car with branches?

-I am sad now that I used so much toxic shit to make that thing. Anyway, I had just made the faceted 650 Polygon John Carmack sculpture. It was so perfect, it felt too much like design. To get away from that I began sketching with twigs, and became fascinated by branch castings. So I went for a wireframe portrait of another character – the Lamborghini from Need for Speed. I was also intrigued by cargo cults and their lo-fi simulations of planes with bamboo.

As an artist experimenting with videogames, what's you take on the art market? Are there and interests from collectors and museum to purchase Game Art at all?
- Game Art as a hyped genre had has thankfully died, or transformed into something else, but there have been artists' works that use game development materials acquired by private collectors and cultural institutions for years now. I have worked with a gallery for the past 5 years. It is how I make a living, but the market is just one piece of a larger constellation.

The interview took place in May 2010.

Suzanne Treister: "Videogame paintings" (1988-)

"Suzanne Treister (b.1958 London UK) studied at St Martin's School of Art, London (1978-1981) and Chelsea College of Art and Design, London (1981-1982), is now based in London having lived in Australia, New York and Berlin. Primarily a painter through the 1980s, Treister was a pioneer in the digital/new media/web based field from the beginning of the 1990s, developing fictional worlds and international collaborative organisations.
Treister's practice deals with notions of identity, history, power and the hallucinatory. Her investigations into the life and research of the fictional character Rosalind Brodsky, most recently explored in the multi-venue project, HEXEN 2039, were described by Art in America as 'One of the most sustained fantasy trips of contemporary art', which belies a deeper mission: to explore how we make sense of history and the politics of war." from artist's homepage

Suzanne, you're considered one of the first artists who fully embraced gaming as a form of artistic expression. How and when did you begin to explore this medium for means different from pure entertainment? And what did you find fascinating about videogames?
-From the mid to late 1980s I spent several nights a week hanging out in amusement arcades in London's Soho with my boyfriend who was hooked on videogames. Over time, waiting around for him to finish so we could go and eat or see a film, I started to think about the games, their structures, their objectives, their themes, their addictiveness. I started to consider their cultural subtexts, antecedents, the effect they may have on society and how they might develop and connect to other mechanisms, developments and fantasies or projections of the future. At first I wasn't so crazy about playing the games myself, until I got addicted to Tetris, and then when I got my Amiga computer in 1991 I started playing some of the platform games, similar to the ones in the arcades, which had come free with the games magazines I was buying for research. In 1995 when I visited Los Angeles for the first time, staying with friends for a week, I barely left the house. I spent almost the whole

time killing and escaping from the Nazis and their dogs in the videogame Castle Wolfenstein, which my hosts were also hooked on.

Did you create your first game-inspired paintings back in the '80s? Why did you decide to transfer digital interactions on a canvas? What games did you find most inspiring?
- Yes, just to backtrack a moment, in the 80s, before I became interested in videogames, I made paintings using appropriated imagery from history and popular culture to describe hypothetical narratives, or possible ways of reading the world. An early series had used themes and imagery relating to the USSR/Russia whilst other works referenced literature, art history, war and religion in the mapping of imaginary scenarios. I saw them as a form of contemporary history painting. On one level much of this work originated from a desire to negotiate my family history, specifically the issues and historical events surrounding the relocation of my father from Poland/France to the UK during WWII which in turn inevitably produced a fascination with the Cold War and the Eastern Bloc. By the end of 1987 my paintings had begun to develop a more repetitive visual structure, images such as books spines, candles, metal bolts and flourescent lights were repeated in rows, blocks or mazes, housing other images or scenes. These works sometimes referenced ludic structures as ways of mapping space and encouraging the viewer's interaction in a psychological sense.
In 1988 I made the first videogame paintings, substituting the characters or forms found in arcade games for historical characters or living persons and everyday objects.
For example, 'Koons Kiefer Videogame' made in 1989 represented the US artist Jeff Koons as a kitsch toy horse about to enter the space of German artist Anselm Kiefer, depicted as a virtual forest of birch trees made up of end to end painted book spines. The inclusion of 'Videogame' in the title aimed to provoke an anticipation of a goal oriented narrative at play, and in the case of the painting, and other related works to come, the development and outcome of this narrative was to be projected by the viewer.

The second painting in the series was titled, 'Videogame for Primo Levi'. Levi was an author I admired, writing about his survival of the Holocaust. I set up the structure of the painting/game as a maze of bolts and hinges through which clusters of green light bulbs had to make their way. The painting was stylistically overtly kitsch, but monumental in scale and reference, highlighting the problematics of artistic representations of history in relation to the corresponding horrific actuality of events, and in turn commenting on the anaesthetising effect of the video game narratives, which were based for the most part on the idea of continuous killing or destruction in the pursuit of an ultimate and singular goal.

Were there other artists around at that time also interested in creating art inspired by videogames? Or did you feel that you were somehow alone in your exploration?
-In the 80s there were no artists I knew of who were interested in making work about videogames and curators who visited my studio didn't even know what they were. Nor did there seem to be any interest in the subject from within academia, although this changed abruptly a few years later with the expansion of the cultural studies industry.
Also at the time of making my first digital works I felt quite alone. In 1991 when artist friends came to my studio and I showed them for the first time my Amiga computer humming on the paint stained workbench they would ask worriedly, 'Of course you'll only be using it to work out your paintings, won't you?' I was severely warned of the dangers of being 'taken over by the machine'. There seemed to be a misconception that the computer actually made the work, rather than the artist, and one could partly blame this on the term 'computer generated' which seemed to have mysteriously entered the language.
I wasn't seduced as such by video games or computers but I felt I had to deal with them as they were not going to go away. I had been however, since childhood, seduced by science fiction, from the British TV series 'Doctor Who', 'The Tomorrow People', 'Adam Adamant Lives', to the writing of George Orwell, H. G. Wells and J. G. Ballard. These, along with writers who interested me several

years later, for example Bulgakov, Bassani, Umberto Eco, Borges, Bruno Schulz and William Gibson, plus my interest in psychoanalytic theory and obsession with the Holocaust and Eastern Europe, all these I would say in one way or another, however oblique, contributed to my move into the new media world, and within that, more explicitly, to a belief in the idea that narrativity and 'reality' was becoming fluid and mutable within these new technologies, and to a suspicion that somehow the 'interactive' video game was an early embodiment of a whole new paradigm which needed to be observed and interrogated.

Between 1991-92, you created a series of fictional videogame stills using Amiga's Deluxe Paint II, and, between 1993-94, you produced "Software", a series of 36 imaginary software packages. What was the idea behind these fictional games?
- The works I made on the Amiga computer were similar to the recent paintings but now incorporated digital effects, text and inevitably resembled far more closely the games themselves. The titles of the works echoed the game titles on the screen. Eg. Are you Dreaming?, Dream Monster, Easyworld 5, Examine the Evidence, Have you been sentenced to a fate worse than death? You have reached the Gates of Wisdom - Tell us what you have seen, Incidents reported, Do you know? Lost in Space, Blinded by the Text, Monster Visions/Song Titles, Identify the Murder Weapon, Mutant Territories-Grand Prix, Quiz 2, No Quiz, Quiz - 10 Questions.
In Mutant Territories-Grand Prix the screen showed an ariel view of a racetrack made of jewles and the instructions on the screen read, 'Drive around the map until you run out of petrol', rather than the usual goal oriented challenge of regular games.
Text was able to enter the works in an organic sense, in that the computer screen was a natural site of text; word processing, text messages, programming. All these manifest text on the screen and I could play on this directly in the works whilst intimating broader subtextual narratives and readings.
Easyworld 5 contained only text instructions. In front of a royal blue curtain appeared the words: Determine your position on the screen and proceed at an even pace. So long as you know where you are

you will be ok. Wait until you have decided where you want to go first. When you have made your decision move player 1 into a vacant box. Then the curtain will open slowly to reveal the object of your dreams. Wait for a few seconds and then press "EXIT". You will have arrived at the scene of a crime. Welcome to Easyworld 5.

Rather than depict the usual suspects from actual games, or versions thereof, in many cases the scenarios were abstracted so that the viewer would have to insert their own hypothetical narrative and become themselves the protagonist, i.e. they would have to imagine their own persona rather than being given the role of a fighter or comic character.

I photographed these early Amiga works straight from the screen. The photographs perfectly reproduced the highly pixilated, raised needlepoint effect of the Amiga screen image. Conceptually this means of presentation was appropriate in that it made it seem like I had gone into a videogame arcade and photographed the games there, lending authenticity to the fictions.

In 1992 I worked on a new Amiga based series which presented stills from a single imaginary videogame. This piece played on the phenomenon of computer system messages counterpoised with the cultural fear/fantasy of a technological future paradise. Individual screen texts read in sequential order: Would you recognise a Virtual Paradise?, Not enough Memory for operation, Presume Virtual Breakdown, You have entered a Virtual Wilderness, Software Failure..., Error finding Question, No Message – Proceed.

Between 1993-94 I made a series of fictional software boxes, each cardboard box and floppy disc label painted to describe an imaginary game or piece of software where various things may happen, where a whole range of virtual experiences could be possible, from pornography to perpetual paranoia, from ethical hallucinations to torture.

Have you ever felt the desire to join the game industry or create art games? Can you share something about Rosalind Brodsky, a virtual persona that is responsible for a remarkable amount of your artistic production? What's the story behind her conception? How is Rosalind connected to gaming?

- No, I never had the ambition to join the gaming industry but I did make a game. From 1997-99 I developed, in line with the developing games industry an interactive cd rom, 'No Other Symptoms – Time Travelling with Rosalind Brodsky', which in many ways echoed the structure of quest games such as Myst. I invented Rosalind Brodsky as an alter ego in 1995 and firstly I made her a set of time travelling costumes. The original biography of Brodsky went like this: 'Rosalind Brodsky, with whom I share Anglo/Eastern European/Jewish roots, was born in London in 1970 and survived until 2058. Her first 'delusional' experience of time travel supposedly occurred while she was in the middle of a session with the pyschoanalyst Julia Kristeva in Paris, at the moment she noticed the similarity of Kristeva's face to the photographic portrait of her Polish-Jewish grandmother who had been murdered in the Holocaust. By 1995 Brodsky is a delusional time traveller who believes herself to be working in London at the Institute of Militronics and Advanced Time Interventionality (IMATI) in the 21st century. IMATI is a controversial government funded organisation which develops equipment and carries out time travel research projects whose results are for use primarily by the military and other government research organisations. Established in 2004 its mission is to carry out interventional historical, anthropological and scientific research through means of time travel. Working with virtual technologies which render the users' bodies invisible in their own time and space the Institute develops virtual simulations of key moments in history. Researchers at the Institute then carry out simulated interventions/experiments within these virtual times/worlds. In academic circles there is controversy as to the validity of this form of 'anthropological' research, but there are many who suspect that IMATI has actually found the secret of authentic time travel.

The cd rom journey takes the form of a tour organised by IMATI in memory of Brodsky's contribution to time travel research. In the introductory scene there is an announcement that a demonstration of armed academics is taking place outside the institute, threatening the building, staff and visitors within. You, the player, now risk remaining in suspended time travel for the rest of your life.

The aim is to survive by navigating the space of Rosalind Brodsky, with escape eventually only possible via her satellite spy probe from where a shuttle will transport you back to earth to an underground home in the mining town of Coober Pedy, South Australia, in the present day.

The tour uncovers biographical and historical data focussing on much of her life, work and personal interests. During her lifetime Brodsky carried out major research in areas of film, TV, music, architecture, genetics, the history of Eastern Europe, the Holocaust, the 1960s and the Russian Revolution as well as contributing to the research and design of a range of time travel equipment. From Brodsky's study, concealed behind a memorial wall, you are able to travel to her home in Bavaria, journey from there to her Satellite in outer space (constructed from Christo's wrapped Reichstag, teleported by IMATI from Berlin in 1995), access her electronic time travelling diary, her feature vibrators and discover the time travelling costumes and attaché cases in her wardrobe. The wardrobe conceals the entrance to a lift which takes you down to the Clinics. The Clinics is an underground laboratory where, for analysis, due to the decline of psychoanalysis in the twenty first century, stressed time travellers must travel back in time to the homes of Freud, Jung, Klein, Lacan and Kristeva. Brodsky's case histories with these analysts are documented as are recordings of her time travelling cookery TV show and the music videos of her band who were popular in Eastern Europe in the 2030s.

The cd rom was completed and published with a book in 1999.

Since then I have not made any games based works except for the inclusion of three video 'training demos' in the 2009 project 'MTB [Military Training Base]' which used footage of actual geographical sites; Donald Judd's ex-military base/art foundation in Marfa, Texas; the ruins of the Palace of the Queen of Sheba in Ethiopia and the Unabomber's cabin in Montana.

Since 2001 I have made works developing from the Brodsky project; documenting and displaying, in installation, web and dvd form, the IMATI Time Travel Research Projects which had supposedly been carried out at IMATI. These include: Golem/Loew - Artificial Life,

Operation Swanlake and HEXEN 2039. I am currently working on the sequel, HEXEN II.

The interview took place in August 2010.

Mauro Ceolin: Emblems and Landscapes

"Mauro Ceolin (Milan, Italy 1963) is a multimedia Italian artist and painter based in Milan, whose work is focused on representing contemporary realities. Since 1996 his research consists in studying the aesthetics forms and the experiences coming from the videogame environments." (from artist's bio)

In your work, you often mix videogames with elements from history. One example is the recurrent use of emblems, which can be found in several paintings from the Middle Ages. You have created an entire series of art games featuring emblems from popular culture, game culture and consumer culture, includin RGBtetris, RGBinvader and RGBwebroids. Why are you so fascinated by emblems?

- Symbols, as letters and words are codes used to express ideas, needs or desires. By using these codes, separating them and putting them together in different ways, I can draw new mental maps that become tools to investigate the every essence of contemporaneity. It is necessary to connect past and future, as no human activity is separated from the previous one, that is to say, one plus one, conventionally, gives as a result two, even though this result is never a given. Talking about the videogames I like to call "paintGame", we have to imagine them as dynamic paintings: as Rembrandt represented a social figure in its "The Night Watch", in RGBinvaders, for instance, I try to show the historical moment in which started the competition between the not open-source OS and Linux. This is what I call a videoludic representation.

The game people series depicts famous people from the videogame industry, including Tomohiro Nishikado (Space Invaders' creator), Dan Houser (vice president of Rockstar Games) and J. Carmack/J. Romero (the designers behind the Doom series). Portraiture of the rich and famous is a very common theme in art history. Why did you choose these subjects, and what do they represent for you?

-One of my first researches for the online project, which dates to the early Zeros, was the portrait series "GamePeople". Around that time, my friend Matteo Bittanti, selected my vectorial drawings for the cover design of an academic book series titled "Ludologica" and later "Videoludica". My intuition, though, began somewhere else: representing the soul of the videoludic world through its creators rather than products. This change of perspective means to show a new kind of reality, different from the physical on, that has as a subject a contemporaneity mediated by new medias. In the "solidLandscape" series, this shift is shown in a deeper way. Here are some relevant criticism: Ludologica, Net Art review, New York Arts Magazine, Domenico Quaranta, Videoludica.

These portraits are created with Flash. Why did you choose this software and not, for example, Photoshop? What do practices like painting and drawing mean to you in the digital age?
- I chose Flash in order to keep the meaning of drawings and their medium of origin and existence somehow coherent. Additionally, Flash gave me the opportunity increase the size of the drawings without compromising their quality.

The notion of landscapes play a central role in your production, as it transpires from the very titles of some of your most celebrated series: promotionalLandscape, solidLandscape and debugLandscape. This is another common trope in art history. And yet, your landscapes are somehow peculiar: you depict the buildings of famous computer and internet corporations but also gamespaces. Do you think our own idea of landscape has changed after the advent of online worlds? Have videogames changed the very idea of how o imagine and represent a landscape? Above all, why are you exploring the digital landscape?
-The idea of landscape didn't change with the appearance of online worlds. The real change took plance with the incorporation of new media in everyday' s life: showing a traditional shape it was possible to me to show a much deeper shift in its meaning. This idea represented a starting point for these three series, focusing on three different shades, all belonging to the contemporary times:

promotionalLandscape examined the design and the architecture of the HQs of key companies of the digital age; solidLandscape investigates the landscapes of videogames and debugLandscape, in a more conceptual way, wonders about the possible role of painting, here compared to a computer debug, in raising key issues of contemporaneity, such as ecology.

What is Bomb Fusion?
-While hiking in the Summer 2005, I discovered some bomb fragments dating back to WW1, in a furious battle that took place in the Alps. I collected these pieces and I melted them down in order to make a sculpture representing the logo of a video-game named "Delta Force: Urban Warfare". This sculpture draws together two different elements of war, one belonging to the past (the bomb's fragments) and one belonging to the present (the video-game logo), creating in this way a temporary synopsis.
"During Summer 2005, while following a hiking trail to Punta Albiolo m. 2969 (Adamello-Presanella Mountains, Italy), I found a piece of a First World War mortar fire (1915-1918). I then engraved on it (with a CNC machine) a vectorial drawing of a landscape taken from "Gran Theft Auto" videogame.With this work I want to represent in one object, different forms of hostility of two historic periods: beginning of XX and beginning of XXI century." (Mauro Ceolin)

When did you become interested in using digital games as a means of artistic expression and intervention?
- In the last ten years my work focused on the analysis of videogames world, in all its facets. This research, represented by the biggest part of my production, sees the videogame not as commercial product but as an important means of expression, both cultural and aesthetic. I had the proof of how big was the influence of videoludic world at one of my first exhibition, when the youngest visitors recognized a painting taken from the SolidLandscape series as a familiar landscape, corroborating, in this way, the idea of shifting the artistic sight "from the window to the computer desktop". Today, having spent ten years representing the contemporary's cultures, starting from representing videoludic

landscapes to showing musicians using videogames consoles in occasion of musical happenings, I began a new meta-scientific project titled contemporaryNaturalism which aims at cataloguing all the "CHARACTERS? VA BN?" living in our collective imaginaries, combining representation and description in a single research.

The interview took place in August 2010.

Chad Chatterton: "Acmipark" (2001-2002)

"Chad Chatterton is an Environment Artist currently living in Australia. He has contributed to various Art Game projects as well as building environments for Funcom's Age of Conan MMO. Chad has traveled to remote areas of Japan and Europe, researching and photographically documenting both dramatic man-made environments such as Gunkanjima. Most recently he was employed as the Artist in Residence at the world-leading video games research group at ITU." (from artist's bio)

The 200 Gertrude Street Gallery in Melbourne seems to have been an important place for artists experimenting with videogames. Both you, Stephen Honegger and Julian Oliver had exhibitions there in the beginning of 2000. Can you tell me something about the gallery and its relevance for the Australian Game Art scene?
- Well Stephen, Julian and I were friends and in fact all lived together in a warehouse studio setup at one stage, so our connections weren't through the gallery as such, but the gallery was (and still is I presume) an important hub of the Melbourne art scene. It housed a stable of subsidised studios that are available for young artists to apply, and from there you had access, an obligation in fact, to exhibit. But any artist could apply to show at Gertrude Street and it was something of a bridge between the artist run spaces Melbourne is known for, and the the more developed or institutionalised art scene beyond. Visiting curators coming to Melbourne would usually drop in and take a stroll through the studios for example, and there was also a studio set aside for foreign artists who had obtained a residency.

In 2000 Max Delaney was running the show at Gertrude Street and he was very hands on and active at all levels of the art scene. It's largely thanks to him that Gertrude Street was interested in the work we produced. He had read a piece I'd written in Like art magazine and asked if I'd curate a show.

"Acmipark [2001-2002] is a virtual environment that contains a site-specific, multiplayer game-based re-imagining of the Australian Centre for the Moving Image, extending the real world architecture of Federation Square into a fantastic abstraction. Acmipark was a non-commercial public artwork commissioned by the ACMI, built from the ground up using Renderware." (Chad Chatterton)

Together with the other member of selectparks you created acmipark, 2003. Which today is a part of the Australian Centre for the Moving Image collection. Can you tell me some about acmipark and perhaps why it was commissioned by ACMI?
-Julian Oliver was due to deliver a paper at the Royal Melbourne Institute of Technology. At the time we were still riding high on our excitement of Half-Life, and spent a lot of time discussing the untapped potential of game engines. Julian's presentation was directing this discussion towards Architects and Virtual Reality professionals. His point was that the time and money spent on architectural fly-thru's and VR projects was falling short of the potential that game engines offered, saying that game has given us a body in our virtual spaces and as a result we're now experiencing our virtual spaces as places. Places where you can become a local, spatially interacting with actual communities.
For the presentation Julian asked me if I wanted to model something indicative of the points he was making, so I chose to model the Architectural Department where most of the audience spend much of their time. So everyone in the audience was familiar with the space we projected at the presentation and it was a powerful moment for this group of professionals to see a real time rendering of a place they new, with all the freedom of movement a game environment can provide.
Using an elevator in the level we then entered Julian's Qthoth map which represented a degree of abstraction and interaction. It's extremely cool and also operates as a tool for live sound performance.
So we were demonstrating the potential game engines have to simulate the real and also the fantastic, highlighting the bodily dimension and what that body can generate through interactivity, particularly in relation to sound.
Helen Stuckey of the Australian Center of the Moving Image was in the audience and suggested to us that we ought to submit a

proposal to Cinemedia (Digital Media Fund), which funded art projects in Australia related to the screen. Helen is really remarkable and has a great deal to do with the health and interest of the game art scene in Melbourne.

At the time the ACMI was part of a major architectural development in the heart of Melbourne called Federation Square. The idea that we developed was to simulate Federation Square and contextualise it in picturesque park surrounds, complete with interactive sound installations, all of which functioned as an online world that anyone could access for free. In this way acmipark effectively extended the public space of the ACMI.

On another level acmipark was for us where we cut our teeth. It was ridiculously ambitious and it was a sink or swim moment. A moment that lasted 2 years.

When did your interest for videogames and their artistic potential begin?

- For me the overlap of art and game doesn't boil down to any one thing of course, however Julian, Stephen and I did share a significant experience that really nourished our enthusiasm for a good long while. We spent some 24 hours locked away in a computer lab and discovered what it was like to really play Half-Life multiplayer deathmatch. It was a transformative experience to be so utterly submerged in that gamespace together. After that we spoke and thought about gaming and game engines constantly.

I won't attempt to define art on any level but I will say that creating places in game engines, which is what I do, allows you to engage with the details of your surroundings, it's form, color, the way different surfaces react to light, sound and movement, the effects of time. I'm constantly thinking about the construction of landscapes and objects, and the relationships of those objects to their landscapes. It's a practice that positions the world as teacher in a very rich way.

Half-Life wasn't my first experience with gaming of course. My Father was a Computer Science teacher and we always had computers at home when I was growing up. I have fond memories of swapping games at school on data cassettes and floppy discs.

However when I was studying at University I didn't really give much thought to games at all, so seeing Half Life was a kind of homecoming.

One of your first solo exhibitions was World's End –a formal analysis of the graphics of destruction in gaming, at 1st Floor Artist and Writers Space, Melbourne. Can you tell me something about the show and which games/engines/tools did you use to create your artwork?

- I was given a slot at the beginning of 2000 at First Floor Artist's and Writer's Space. It was a last minute thing and was an earlier slot in the Art calendar than usual, meaning they probably just wanted somebody to pay the rent. Whether you take the Christian calendar seriously or not, 2000 was a pretty momentous new year I think you'll agree, so I decided to take it. Exhibitions are like significant diary entries, and I though it would be an interesting time to have a show.

At the time I was living with a guy who, together with his girlfriend, took the Y2K threat very seriously. They were stocking up on long life milk, had even organised a house in the country where they would be safe. (He actually was a big influence on my interest and understanding of gaming, and went on to write for some gaming magazines in the UK. I remember he managed to convince the Melbourne University library to subscribe to Edge magazine). I wanted to feed of of this fear associated with the turn of the century by looking at the graphics of explosions.

In the end I sourced R-Type mostly, which I thought was as beautiful a display of pixels as anything I'd seen. It perfectly occupies that space between symbol and thing, with just enough resolution and color range to become more than the sum of its parts.

The show itself builds on earlier work I did using small concrete blocks that I'd made. I would carry several hundred of these blocks to the gallery and then start playing with them, building these knee high architectural structures in the gallery space. So with World's End I wasn't exactly sure what I was going to build when I started, and for me that was part of the joy.

When I look at the few images I have of the exhibit now I can see that the pieces are just sketches, iterations that might have evolved into a more worthwhile show down the line. But it's an obvious thing do, build with pixel blocks in this way. It's actually a very easy thing to do and, that in itself is pleasurable, but I guess it wasn't what I was looking for.

In the end I realised that this impulse to 'take from game and build in the real world' is flawed and generally not very interesting. A year later I had left Gertrude Street, packed up my studio, materials and tools, and folded everything into a computer where I focused on learning the tools of the game dev trade.

The interview took place in October 2010.

John Paul Bichard: "The White Room" (2004),

"John Paul Bichard is an artist who has worked with digital media, games, photography and installation since the early nineties. He curated and produced On a Clear Day in 1996, a ground breaking digital game art project that took place around the UK. As Mute magazine's games editor from 1995 to 2001, Bichard explored and wrote on the cultural significance of the then emerging video game scene and was invited to show work at the Virtual Architecture exhibition at the ICA in 1998. For the past two years he has been head of interaction with the public authoring digital research project Urban Tapestries a joint venture with France Telecom, HP, Orange and the DTI. He is currently starting a mobile game research project Backseat Gaming with the Interactive Institute mobility studio in Stockholm." (from artist's bio)

You were among the first artists interested in "upgrading" - or at very least, "rethinking" - the medium of photography in the videogame age. How do you explain your fascination for photography and gaming?
- I have had an interest in the 2D pictorial space for years: I enjoyed photos as a kid but didn't have the patience or money to enjoy film rolls and processing, so no romantic stories about developing rolls of film in my parent's bathtub... I went to St Martins art school where I got a degree in painting, then stopped painting but retained an interest in the conceptual 2D planar space that pictures create. I had been playing Dungeons and Dragons since it started and played my first videogame in the '70s: Pong at Southampton airport. It was fascinating and set in motion a slow but enduring chain of events. My interest in video gaming grew through the '80s with a home computer and arcade games, which I couldn't really afford to play so totally sucked at. It wasn't until Doom II came out that I really took a step forward and started the journey I am still on with video games. It fascinated me that believable worlds could be created, that you could be immersed in even a crappy story as long as there was enough action. I started writing for the influential art and

technology paper, Mute and even did a few game reviews for Wired which gave me the excuse to be sent bucketloads of new games as a games editor and reviewer. My interest in writing was to put forward the notion that videogames were a cultural phenomenon and not just a means of stopping teenage boys for jerking off. So I carried on my work as an artist, started a couple of design companies, mainly working with game clients and played a lot of video and computer games. I did one of the first viral marketing campaigns for the launch of Grand Theft Auto 2, did a small viral campaign for Pokemon the movie, Thomas the Tank Engine and a bunch of games that died and were quickly buried. But... the big turning point was Half-Life (the game): a great story where you really felt immersed on a psychological level, as an everyday person, not some over-pumped hero, just a simple and rather inadequate employee expected to save the world. The genius of Half Life was that around the half way mark, you suddenly realised that you had been betrayed, it was a set-up, the people you thought you were running to, were firing at you. That is a moment I will never forget, it still gives me goose bumps.

So I still haven't answered your question - videogames simply became a way of life from quite early on, the 2d pictorial space has also been a place for exploring and understanding the world for as long as I can remember. The two collided when I did an art exhibition in Lisbon: I was invited to show a game I had made: it was a process based work: 'start with an empty 3d space and see how far you get building some kind of game related environment/experience in 90 days' the result was odd - an empty, stacked game world where you could see the levels as you dropped out of them. But when I got to the gallery it was so beautiful, with marble floors and gardens and huge glass windows that I couldn't bear blocking out the world and showing an interactive art work so I talked the director into letting me do an installation: 3 days, chicken blood, police tape, bits of a dead cow, some fabric and a lot of adrenalin and I came up with a real world equivalent of what would happen if you could see a game level at the end of the level, in real life. It was an installation, it stank after 2 days, so I had to photograph it and clean it up. This was the first time I used photography and art and gaming together.

"Evidência takes as its starting point, an ending; a forensic space, a place in which remains and material take on new significance. From the objects and images, there are no definite conclusions, no clear narratives, just the threads of something that could have happened. The viewer is invited in, but in doing so enters the scene to witness part... of a crime, a conflict, a game?" (Jean Paul Bichard)

With "The White Room" (2004), your photographic interventions became more explicit and daring. You toured Max Payne 2, took pictures of the locales and environments, removed the innumerable corpses that furnished those spaces, but left a trace of virtual blood as a memento of past interactions... Why did you specifically choose this action-adventure?

- "The White Room" is complicated. The show was a conceptual response to domesticity and the new wave of art photography called 'The house in the Middle' at Towner Gallery, Eastbourne in England. It was a photographic group show based around notions of post war domesticity and social (mainly class based) constructs, so I was invited to show with British heavyweights like Martin Parr and Richard Billingham. I was meant to do an 'art game' which engaged the conceptual framework of the show but that felt too much like 'token gameart freak show' than a serious reflection on the video game space so I decided to produce a series of photo based objects. My earlier works had explored the relationship between the forensic (crime) space and the violent videogame space: these were still, reflective works that questioned consequence, the nature of violence and violent narrative as well as the aesthetics of violence and blood in particular. These earlier works were also real world explorations that drew inspiration from, queried and de-constructed video games in a real world setting. So I decided to de-construct the violent game space from the inside, from within the game space. I went back through all my then current games and settled upon Max Payne 2, mostly for its social realism, the wonderfully atmospheric interiors and the ability to easily edit the game.

"The White Room is a set of photographic prints resulting from an in-game photo shoot that documents a series of constructed disasters. These interiors were set up by the artist using the videogame Max Payne 2, a 'Film Noir' thriller that tells a tale of lost love, deception and betrayal. The shoot took place within the game's developer mode using the GOD and GETALLWEAPONS cheats and BenDMan'S 'bloody mod 1.2'." (John Paul Bichard)

"The White Room" was for me, a step further: as I was looking through the game for locations that looked like crime scenes, I came across a really bloody game mod that exaggerated the blood stains. So I used the game as a canvas, shooting bodies around a potential crime scene to create grizzly locations. It struck me as I was doing this that I could also arrange the locations, the position of the camera, as I would in a shoot, in other words to treat the game as both a canvas and a photo location. People criticised me at the time for ripping off the game and just taking screen shots, but I was seriously trying to take a step further within the game space and explore my own ideas through the captured image. To a lesser extent, and within the conceptual ambitions of the exhibition, I also used the work as a very oblique and arguably obscure critique of the stereotypical, mildly racist and sexist narratives and tropes that have influenced the very male video game world from the start. Hence the high contrast between the White Room which is a typical white, upper middle class apartment in contrast to the run down black/hispanic/white trash lower class apartments that were present in the game and that arguably reinforce the social prejudices that get propagated in video games. I got permission from the game publisher to use the work but was not allowed to sell them so I have donated a set of the images to the Contemporary Art Museum in Tampa after I showed the works there.

You also participated in the exhibition "Game Art" at Mejan Labs in Stockholm, which remains, as of today, one of the largest exhibitions in Sweden entirely focused on Game Art. How did you get involved in the exhibition? And what was the impact of this event on the Scandinavian Game Art scene?

- Well, I knew Björn Norberg and Peter Hagdahl who were running Mejan Labs through my work at the Interactive Institute. Since coming to Sweden 5 years ago, I have been a games designer and creative/artistic director on four high profile pervasive games at the Institute, games that pull the digital experience into the real world with mobile technologies, live action role playing and narratives devised for the new genre. I think the show was influential within the rather limited media art 'world 'in Sweden but one of the few critics here wrote a very unenlightened (read: bullshit!) review in one of the biggest international art magazines which didn't help expand the scene. This is a criticism I have of the scene here, it is controlled by too few people in influential positions which is disastrous for a small but energetic scene in a small but ambitious country. Mejan sadly ended as it couldn't raise enough funding. The term "Game Art" is problematic, in my opinion it should be seen as part of the wider art scene and not a separate branch, it is 'interesting' but too marginal to be treated as an isolated genre.

"Inverse Forensics utilises movements, methods and behaviours from first person shooter videogame characters and environments to construct an experimental videogame dance performance. The work is centered upon a dancer who assumes the role of the player character: a generic special forces combatant, and her opponent: an implied non player character (invisible) who is revealed only by the gaze of the dancer and the generated blood traces left on the wall post-shooting." (John Paul Bichard)

On the opening evening at Mejan Labs you presented a bold performance piece titled "Inverse Forensics" (2007). What was your intent?

-John Paul Bichard: I was approached initially to do the cast 'Severed Hand' piece which is a lifelike waxwork cast of my hand severed as I hold a computer mouse, but I figured that the show was a great opportunity to do something a bit more ambitious. So six weeks before the opening, I looked around on Myspace for a dancer and found Mira Mutka an excellent Stockholm based contemporary dancer to collaborate with. The process and resulting performances were inspiring and an eye opener. I saw not just my own work but also gaming and male violence from an entirely different perspective. Mira took the role of a special forces operative in a typical seek and destroy scenario. She was playing against an invisible foe with an invisible gun and I showed where the head shots had taken place by splashing theatrical blood onto the walls. What could have been somewhat humorous was in fact tense, powerful and engaging for the audience, many of whom had never played a first-person shooter. I repeated the performance in a different format in Umeå with the hand sculpture and the documentary video which was also shown when the show toured to Piteå.

You are now an artist in residence at the Interactive Institute Art & Technology in Stockholm. What are you working on these days?
- Actually as I sit here writing, I am a freelance creative advisor, working on digital and photographic art installations for property developers around Sweden. I also continue to work as artistic director for a Parkour based pervasive game at the Institute but the Art and Technology department where I was based has been dismantled as it no longer fitted in to the wider research agenda. This is a fairly typical fate for art, which is not a bad thing: art is a catalyst, a flavour, an initiator that moves on once the place they are based in matures. As far as my game art is progressing, well I am working mostly with photography series around identity and roles/role playing so shoot a lot of people in the LARP scene, the burlesque and fetish worlds and a series where I invited people to cover themselves in fake blood in my bath... the ideas continue to draw influence from gaming but perhaps they have grown further towards real games and identities in the real world. I still play role playing games and a wonderful MMO called Dofus but have become somewhat tired of the over-formulaic mainstream game scene - I want games that move beyond simple destroy-for-points mechanics, not that I want to see an end to game violence but rather, more intelligent narratives and mechanics that favour exploration or imaginative solutions to difficult situations... One day...

The interview took place in September 2010.

Rosemarie Fiore: "Arcade Game Photographs" (1980)

Fiore was born in New York State and currently lives and works in New York City. In 2001, Fiore took long exposure photographs of video war games of the 80's created by Atari, Centuri and Taito. As she wrote on her website: "The photographs were shot from video game screens while I played the games. By recording each second of an entire game on one frame of film, I captured complex patterns not normally seen by the eye." This series left a mark in the minds in the emerging game Art scene and forced viewers to rethink the very notion of game photography.

A decade ago you made a series of long exposure photographs of video games of the 1980s by Atari, Centuri and Taito. How and why did you choose these specific arcade titles?
- I took long exposure photographs of 1980 vector-based video games by opening up the shutter as soon as I began the game and closing the shutter when my ship blew up. Sometimes the exposure time lasted for many minutes, other times it lasted for just a few seconds. Each negative recorded a lifetime in cyber space. Before developing the images, I imported them into Photoshop. There, I removed the score and man/ship count leaving just the image extracted from its context. The games I chose to photograph were ones that I played in the 1980s at my local arcade (Gyruss, Quantum, Battlezone, Missile Command, Asteroids, Qix andTempest). I chose them intuitively though many of them had to do with conflict or war.

What is you personal relationships with videogames? Do you consider them a tool for artistic experimentation?
- I had a very typical relationship with video games growing up in the late 1970s and early 1980s. I remember Pong was the first video game I played on our TV. We then got a Magnavox Odyssey. Arcade style video games were pretty much a new thing and large arcades were opening up all over the place. My brother and I would

ride our bikes to the local arcade where we would play for hours. At that time, you could play a long time on one quarter. I'll never forget playing Asteroids for the first time and experiencing zero gravity. It felt so real. I didn't think about video games as an art-making tool or consider the images it could generate until I began exploring this idea in my own work.

Have you worked with videogames in some other forms? Is it something you would like to come back to in the future?
- I would like to return to working with video games in the future. Although the imagery from these long exposure photographs is very present in my work. I see it in the paintings created with a Scrambler amusement park ride as well as my "Firework Drawings". Kinetic painting is a recurrent theme in your works, e.g. pinball paintings, rear wiper and lawn mower paintings.

Why are you fascinated by capturing kinetic traces on your canvas?
- I am interested in marks generated by mechanisms and technology. It is the way I remove my hand from the work and introduce decisions from another source. The other source introduces the unexpected into the work. I then respond in some way. I work collaboratively with the mechanism. We go back and forth. Over time, this is the way the image is constructed. I am presently working the same way with colored smoke bomb fireworks by capturing and composing the movement of the smoke they release on paper.

The interview took place in December 2010.

Katherine Isbister: "SIMBEE" (2004)

Katherine Isbister researchs and design digital games and other computer-supported experiences, focusing on emotion and social connection--understanding the impact of design choices on these qualities, and figuring out how to get better at making and evaluating digital experiences that have these qualities. Isbister is an associate professor at New York University's Polytechnic Institute in Brooklyn, jointly appointed in Digital Media and Computer Science and Engineering. She also maintains an affiliation at the IT University in Copenhagen's Center for Computer Games Research. At NYU-Poly, she directs the Social Game Lab, is an investigator in the NYU Games for Learning Institute, and serves on the Advisory Committee of the NYU Game Center.

When and where did you and Rainey Straus meet? Why did you choose Maxis' The Sims as a platform/canvas/tool for your projects?

-Rainey and I met in San Francisco way back in the '90s, when the internet was still shiny and new :) We worked together on a design project, and found our perspectives and interests were very compatible, and became friends, long before we launched our series ofSims artworks. The first piece, "SimGallery", was in response to a call for works for the Yerba Buena show featuring game art in 2004. We used The Sims Online to establish a portal between the real gallery and a virtual one we'd created in the game, and curated a show of works inside the game, that people could visit from within the game, but also, by sitting down at the exhibition in San Francisco. The game was a perfect tool for creating such a window between worlds, and we knew there were already artists working within the game, and an arts community, that we tapped for the show. We did studio visits within the game to curate the exhibition.

With "SiMBEE" (2004) you mixed Vanessa Beecroft's performances with The Sims. What was the genesis of this project?
- Rainey did this work--there's a lot of player-created content and hacking that happens with the Sims, and she found tools online that players had created, that allowed her to take imagery from Beecroft's installations and craft Sims that recreated the look of the models used in that work. We did a lot of this kind of modding/hacking for our "SimVeillance": the San Jose piece as well.

In your Sims-based projects you are exploring the boundaries between reality and virtuality. This quest for authenticity, if you will, seems to be the main theme of such installations as "SimGallery" and "SIMVeillance"?
- Games invite our participation and projection--we are actors in these virtual spaces, and they are such plastic, malleable worlds. They are a tremendously powerful venue for exploring issues of representation, of identity, of control of our own image, as well as issues of aesthetics and how our senses are framed by the context in which we experience art. The Sims itself is a world in which these kinds of explorations are happening on a mass scale for everyday consumers, and was a ripe context for conducting such investigations.

SIMveillance is very interesting as it explores the ideology of surveillance in both real and virtual worlds...
- This piece was actually about how we're monitored in real life--we hooked up surveillance/security cameras outside the San Jose Museum of Art, and used the footage of passers-by to then create Sims in their likeness that we inserted into our recreation of that plaza within the Sims 3 (n.B. this project had a lot of assist from Chelsea Hash, a student of mine at the time who is now a freelance game artist/designer).
"SimVeillance" was giving these traces of those who passed by a peculiar kind of 'life of their own', within the game simulation world. I think this is comparable to your digital traces on the web--how your history in terms of blogging, websites, Facebook, twitter, and the like gets 'legs' and can get away from you, can develop its

own sort of existence. We were making this very obvious and visual, with what we did, and immediate, in the sense that when you saw the piece inside the San Jose Museum of Art, you might realize "Oh, I was just there! I wonder if I'm in the game now..." It's interesting to realize that we leave traces of ourselves in so many places, that can be used to so many purposes, in this digital age. Definitely this piece was examining/drawing attention to this.

What is your personal relationship to videogames? How do you see art and digital gaming connecting in the future?
-Games are the object of my research and they are also a passion in the sense that I see them as a potent driver of the future of how we'll engage with tech and with one another. I think artists will use games as a medium and as a subject of investigation for many years to come, as they are such a potent force in the culture now, and also, are at the vanguard of our crafting of mediated experience. I'm sure Rainey would have thoughts about this as well.

The interview took place in December 2010.

Ben Chang: "Philosopher DeathMatch" (2006)

"Ben Chang is an electronic artist whose work explores the intersections of virtual environments and experimental gaming with contemporary media art. Using materials ranging from immersive visualization systems to modified surveillance cameras, hacked video games, and antique telegraphs, his work brings out the chaotic, human qualities in technological systems. His installations, performances, and immersive virtual reality environments have been exhibited in numerous venues and festivals worldwide, including Boston CyberArts, SIGGRAPH, the FILE International Electronic Language Festival in Sao Paulo, the Athens MediaTerra Festival, the Wired NextFest, and the Vancouver New Forms Festival, among others. He has designed interactive exhibits for museums such as the Museum of Contemporary Art, Chicago, and the Field Museum of Natural History. He is an Associate Professor in the Department of the Arts and Co-Director of the Games and Simulation Arts and Sciences Program at Rensselaer Polytechnic Institute." (from the artist's homepage)

When did your fascination for videogame begin? What do you find particularly interesting abouit the medium?
- I'm part of what's sometimes called "the gamer generation," so I grew up with videogames. I think our individual understanding of games is informed by our moment of first exposure - for me, the starting points are early games on the Timex-Sinclair 1000, then the Apple II, and then of course the NES. I got into programming at a pretty early age, but it wasn't actually game programming that got me started. I did try writing games – I remember working my way through this big book which would teach you AppleSoft BASIC to build this rudimentary space shoot-em-up. It was incredibly boring and I never made it all the way through; I think I gave up somewhere in the chapter where you had to manually type in pages of machine code in hex for some assembly-optimized sprite-blitting routine.
The thing that got me hooked on programming was actually fractals. The idea that you could create this tiny program to generate such

beautiful, infinitely complex worlds was mind-blowing. The qualities that drew me deep into the Mandelbrot Set night after night are actually still at the core of a lot of my work today. One is the idea of emergent behavior, creating complex interactions and experiences from the system of relations between different elements. Another is the act of encounter with strange terrain, a kind of sensation of space verging on the sublime, that I'm seeking through installation or through immersive virtual environments. I see this thread connecting William Gibson's luminous vision of cyberspace and the Situationists' psychogeography, along with the tendrils of Mandelbrot's canyons being etched out in ghostly green monochrome, one pixel at a time.

My return back to videogames as a creative medium has been through interactive digital art, first as a kind of found object to be hacked and modified, and more recently as a unique form which is deeply interconnected with interactive art.

In "Philosopher DeathMatch" (2006), a Quake III modification, the players are playing the role of famous philosophers. What was your criteria for selecting the initial roster of philosophers? Are there any connections between their discourse and gameplay?
- The starting point for "Philosopher Deathmatch" was the idea of abstracting the game to get at its essence beneath the visual representation. Super Mario Brothers, for example, looks like it's about a rotund Italian plumber jumping on turtles and mushrooms, but like so many truly great games it's really about this fluid choreography of timing, rhythm, reaction, and memory. Quake III Arena was a landmark game in the multiplayer first-person-shooter genre, known for the pure distillation of reflex aggression. I was interested in the idea of taking this system of violence and imagining what else it could be used to represent, which led me to philosophy as the most absurdly opposite human activity to twitch gaming. As it turns out, the feedback I got from professional philosophers was that this is actually not that absurd at all – they felt it was a pretty good representation of the no-holds-barred intellectual combat that philosophy is actually all about.

The philosophers are a bit of an idiosyncratic mix. Obviously Socrates and Plato have to be in there. Heidegger is crucial, for his fixation on a fundamental understanding of the nature of being (dasein), which is applicable first because of question of virtual being, and second because in Q3A you spend a lot of time flickering between being and not-being whenever you get fragged. Bertrand Russell is maybe the counter to Heidegger's mysticism. Nietzsche's thought is pretty central to the game, in terms of nihilism and morality and particularly his idea of the "will to power." Descartes, for the Cartesian grid and the mind-body duality which the piece is partly about overcoming. Jeremy Bentham is there for his invention of the panopticon, which via Foucault has of course become a dominant trope in critical theory, particularly around contemporary media.

Philosophers are sometimes surprised that he's a playable character; while he's an important figure in utilitarianism he's not usually thought of as a household name. He's also known for his "auto-icon," a hay-stuffed likeness originally made with his actual skeleton and mummified head, seated in a glass-fronted cabinet at the University College in London. The gruesome, monstrous characters in the original Quake III Arena seem pretty normal by comparison. I've been occasionally adding more every so often (Deleuze was the latest), but there are so many more philosophers who should be added to the player roster through expansion packs; Merleau-Ponty, Liebniz, Hume, Rousseau, Marx, Husserl, Spinoza, Donna Haraway, Katherine Hayles, Brian Massumi, Ian Bogost ...

In 2002 you created a game and a performance called "Guitar Gods", which reminds me of Activision's popular music game Guitar Hero. It is almost a prefiguration. How did you come up with "Guitar Gods"?
- Guitar Gods was a piece that I made with Dima Strakovsky and the late Chris Sorg, initially as part of a larger multi-format project called The Jackals. This was a combination of hacker workshops, installation, and performance, created by a group called TangentLab that included Andrew Sempere, Mary Lucking, Silvia Ruzanka, Rodger Ruzanka, and any friends or bystanders that we could rope

in. The basic idea to scavenge and repurpose old and obsolete technology and create something new. Often these were parodies of current technologies, like the "PDA (Personal Data Annoyance)", which is like a PalmPilot but the size of a briefcase, with a loud droning computer voice reciting an infinite list of appointments, news items, and stock quotes.

I guess that joke doesn't work anymore, since the PalmPilot is just as obsolete as the Powerbook 180 we scavenged to run the thing in the first place. For a Jackals event we would basically improvise things like this, or the "Data Weather Balloon" or the "JackalVision Mobile Videoconferencing Suit," in a kind of open-studio format that would also include things like basic electronics workshops for the public. Our costumes consisted of clean-room suits and jackal masks made of hand-woven wire and electronics components. This was around 2002-2003, at the cusp of this current huge wave of DIY / circuit-bending/hacker/maker culture. "Guitar Gods" came out of The Jackals and then evolved into a standalone piece. It's primarily an interactive piece, but we used it for a circuit-bending / electro-noise performance at the all-night Summer Solstice event at the Museum of Contemporary Art in Chicago.

Did you ever regret the fact that you never produced a commercial version of "Guitar Gods" to compete with Guitar Hero?
- "Guitar Gods" and Guitar Hero both use similar controllers, though ours was made by hacking cheap electronic toys from the thrift store. There are some important differences, though. The first is that "Gods" are, obviously, much more awesome than "Heros." The other difference is that Guitar Hero is a rhythmic pattern-following game, basically like Simon (or like Super Mario Brothers, but much more linear), which uses music as the output of the scoring system. Guitar Gods, on the other hand, is a little less like a game and more like a musical instrument, albeit one that probably gives you more the experience of being Christian Marclay than Jimi Hendrix.

I don't know if "Guitar Gods" would be easy to commercialize; it also relies heavily on appropriation and subversive parody of the entire rock/metal genre that it simultaneously revels in. Now, of course, ActiVision has discontinued the series, so Guitar Hero itself joins the world of the obsolete for the next generation.

As a college professor, have you noticed any patterns or trends in your students' experimentations with game-based technology? What is their main interest nowadays?

- The biggest change over the last ten years has probably been in the level of sophisticated tools that students and independent game developers have at their disposal. This means that you don't have to spend nearly as much time re-inventing the wheel and building basic things from scratch, and can get to the actual creative process much quicker. The priority for game engines used to only be about performance, like graphics quality.

Now there's a whole host of engines, like Unity3D, which are still very sophisticated but are also designed to be easier to use and more affordable and are aimed at students and indie developers. There's also a strong community of Free/Open-Source tools, like Panda3D, Irrlicht, OGRE, PyGame and Blender. There's a democratization of tools. Closing the gap of technology cost and production value means that there are fewer practical barriers in getting started developing games, which means there can be more independent voices in the mix. It's also much easier to prototype, sketch, and iterate. I can give students a project like "Three-Hour Game Jam" or some oblique, conceptual weekly assignment and they can produce games that are completely functional and also thought-provoking.

From your vantage point, what do you think the future of interactive media on our culture is going to look like?

-I think the only thing we can predict is a continuing emergence of the unexpected. Interactivity introduces a significant change from most existing media forms. The superficial ways in which we often think about incorporating it frequently fail, while success comes from unlikely directions. We expected interactive movies, which haven't really happened; instead we have World of Warcraft, FarmVille, Passage, and Minecraft. Interactivity as an aesthetic dimension is not new, but certainly still has plenty of room to develop and mature. I see a lot of promise in the world of indie game development, and also the kinds of changes going on in the game industry as a whole, from physical interfaces to mobile and social gaming.

Working with interactivity in art context allows certain kinds of experimental freedoms, but at the same time there are other limitations imposed. Working in games allows a different set of experimental freedoms. One thing that's clear is that interactivity as a medium cannot be reduced to or contained within any existing media – for example, witness the mountain of games that fail abysmally because they try to be cinema. Myron Krueger put forward the idea of interactivity as an art form, which to me is always something connected to all other media yet also distinct, a rhizomatic that winds its way between far-flung historical moments and high and low cultural forms.

It's hard to make predictions very far into the future, but a few trends I see are the continuing advancement of augmented reality and pervasive computing, the spread of physical and gestural interfaces, renewed interest in immersive virtual environments due to radically cheaper technology. In terms of content there's real drive in the industry to make games that are smarter, deeper, and more interesting. More importantly, the rise of an indie and DIY game development culture means that we will see generations of not just game players but game creators.

The interview took place in October 2011.

Antoinette LaFarge: "Plaintext Players" (1994)

Antoinette LaFarge is an American new media artist and professor of Digital Media at University of California Irvine. She was among the first artists to choose online performance as her means of expression in the emerging world of the web. Together with Robert Niedeffer, LaFarge curated one of the first collective exhibitions entirely devoted to Game Art. Titled "SHIFT-CTRL: Computers, Games & Art", the event took place at the Beall Center for Art and Technology, in UC Irvine's University Gallery, and on the Internet in 2000.

In 1994, you founded Plaintext Players, an online performance group inspired by MOOs text-based online experiences. Where did you get the inspiration to create a series of performances in virtual spaces?
-I got involved with MOOs in early 1994 while I was in graduate school. I was initially entranced by the immersive quality of these spaces and the way they straddled a line between performing and being, and between writing and doing. From the outset I had a strong impulse to play in MOO, to make up stuff, to not take part under my own name and history. Some of my fellow students had a similar impulse, and at first we would just meet up online and improvise very loosely. For instance, we might change our avatar names (@rename) 4 or 5 times an hour just to prod each other to change how we were interacting. We were the puppetmasters and the puppets.
From that, it seemed an obvious step to try to organize the spontaneous performances in a way that would highlight what I saw to be the affordances of MOO (role play, fluidity of language, polyphonic discourse, group invention) and downplay some of the issues (spamming, incoherence). So I started writing scenarios for the group to structure the improvisations, and I started live-directing the pieces as they unfolded.

Were the performances somehow connected to early text-based adventures such as Colossal Cave or Zork?
-At that time, I had not yet begun playing computer games to any great extent, so there was no direct influence from any of the early text-based adventure games or even from MOOs' first cousins, the MUDs. I was influenced much more by my (admittedly limited) history of working with live performance and my growing interest in traditional forms of improvisation. And even more by the tradition of gamelike activities in 20th century art— Marcel Duchamp channeling Rrose Sélavy, Marcel Broodthaers pretending to be a museum all by himself, Lynn Hershman creating her Roberta Breitmore alter ego. But one of the things that kept me going was that none of the rules of either performance or writing mapped perfectly over to this new space—indeed, this was the primary factor that convinced me it was a genuinely new art medium. For instance, unlike theater, there were no physical limits on what the characters could 'do', and it was much easier to enact doppelgangers and other kinds of doubling. The performed texts were much closer, grammatically, to spoken than to written language even though they appeared in the form of writing. We had to experiment extensively to determine what worked and what didn't—we could take almost nothing for granted. I should add that part of this experimentation involved working with code—reprogramming MOO to better support the work—though this level of activity remained almost entirely invisible to our audiences.

GameScenes: How did you publicize your performances and events? Back then the pool of potential participants and spectators must have been quite small...

Antoinette LaFarge: The group I founded, the Plaintext Players, was limited by (a) who was online at that early stage in the evolution of the internet, (b) who was interested in live role play in a text-based environment, and (c) who knew about us (or whom I could recruit). That meant that most of my early performers were either artists and writers I knew offline or other inhabitants of MOOs, especially people I met on either LambdaMOO or PMCMOO.

Our audiences were of two kinds: those who congregated in our on-MOO performance space (usually no more than a few dozen) and those who watched our performances in 'real world' spaces through large-scale projections. These were set up at places like art galleries, universities, or conferences, and I (or occasionally one of the other performers) would usually be physically present at the location, in order to talk to the audience afterward about what was happening. At that time, most of our audience was extremely puzzled about what was going on with the scrolling text that they saw as our performance took place. Was it live? Was it computer-generated? Where were the people? Were common questions. These audiences ranged from a few dozen to several thousand. We spread the word through email listservs as well as through traditional publicity materials like postcards, flyers, posters, and so on.

For how long did you perform online? What was the next step?
- We did these kinds of performances for several years. This was around the same time as Adriene Jenik and Lisa Brenneis were doing performance interventions in the Palace, and the Hamnet Players were working in IRC channels. I think that the artistic potential of social environments has not yet developed to its full—though such efforts continue, primarily in Second Life—in part because the culture moved too quickly to map normative behaviors onto these pseudonymous environments. In other words, they didn't treat them as fundamentally theatrical and fictional (as I did)—that is, as areas formally marked off for play—but as analogous to or extensions of ordinary social space. A good deal of the contest over Facebook, I think, arises from this very tension. We're still learning, in effect, how to create and live with a playful social space.

Anyway, a little after that, around the mid-1990s, I got interested in mixing online performers (like the Plaintext Players) with 'real space' actors. All performance is essentially artifice, no matter now 'natural' we try to make it look, so I thought it would be pretty interesting to bring together a group of performers used to working deeply through their bodies with another group whose physical bodies remained ancillary to their performances. Beginning with Still Lies Quiet Truth in 1997, and then more ambitiously with the two Roman Forum projects (2000, 2003) and Demotic (2004,

2006), I started integrating these two universes through different channels: live text, computer-generated text, live audio, synthetic audio, live video, canned video, etc.

These performances took on a gamelike quality in that they were all structured to some degree around improvisations on varying sets of rules and goals. It was really driven by an aesthetic of limitations— one group not being able to see the other, who maybe couldn't hear the first. I got sick of people assuming that working with "just text" (or "just" anything) was a bandwidth issue— when it wouldn't occur to them to ask Herman Melville, for example, if he didn't think Moby Dick would be so much better with pictures.

"Christmas" was Plaintext Players' first set of performances. How did the series develop over time? Was it heavily scripted or was it mostly improvised?

-The Christmas series of 19 performances were all based on a very short scenario entitled Christmas: Ein Schauspiel that my longtime collaborator, the director Robert Allen, had written a couple of years earlier for no particular reason. I had just started looking for ways to develop my group's improvisational methods, and Robert offered us the scenario as a possible basis for more structured work. Robert also took part as a performer in some of the Plaintext Players pieces.

Why did Robert's scenario appeal to you?

- Robert's scenario seemed ideal to me because it was a very simple story with three archetypal figures in an unresolved relationship: there's Big Man, who occasionally gets so angry he runs amok; there's Little Man, his keeper and friend, who tries to keep Big Man in control; and then there's Bloody Zelda, who is always trying to push Big Man to extremes. (Bloody Zelda's name was not based on the Legend of Zelda character, by the way; it's just one of those coincidences.) Using this trio as the key, I wrote detailed scenarios for each of the 19 performances that developed their relationships in various ways.

Even with written scenarios as a guide, every performance would develop in wholly unexpected ways, and this unpredictability remained hugely appealing to all of us and was a major factor in keeping the Plaintext Players going as long as they did in their 'obsolete media' corner of the internet. In one memorable performance, for example, BloodyZelda and LittleMan went to court to battle over legal custody of BigMan, but their trial was invaded and almost completely derailed by an assortment of characters from the then-recent O.J. Simpson murder trial.

"SHIFT-CTRL: Computers, Games & Art" is remembered today as one of the first exhibitions entirely devoted to Game Art in the United States. What was your goal, as a co-curator? What were the selection criteria that you and Robert Nideffer select?
- Both Robert Nideffer and I believed that computer games showed enormous potential as a rising art form, and we wanted to highlight what we thought were the most interesting kinds of work being done, as a pointer to the future. Even then, it was clear to us that the computer game industry was following the trajectory of the movie industry—from independent artists to megacorporations—but in a much compressed time frame, and that this would drastically limit the range and quality of what could be produced. So we thought it was important to highlight some of the paths gaming could take that didn't just lead to a thousand cookie-cutter versions of Doom aimed at a single demographic (young American men). We chose three areas we were particularly excited about to focus on: role-playing games and environments; AI-based and game-like systems; and user-generated software hacks.
We also wanted to underline that computer games don't exist in a cultural vacuum but are part of a much larger and richer history of games and their overlap with the fields of visual art, performance, design, and literature. The essay I wrote for the show, WinSide Out reflects this point of view and was intended to serve as a kind of primer for people new to the idea that games and art had a large zone of intersection.
One of the things I'm especially proud of is our inclusion in this show of a number of artists who were pioneers in the field and have since become well-known names: Perry Hoberman; Natalie Bookchin; RTMark; Eddo Stern; Negativland; jodi.org; Rebecca

Allen; Mongrel; Christa Sommerer; Adriene Jenik; Lev Manovich; Ken Feingold; Eric Zimmerman.

The follow-up exhibition, "ALT+CTRL", took place in 2004 at the Beall Center for Art + Technology at UC Irvine. How did Game Art evolve during that interval?
-What mainly happened in those four years was that the Hollywoodization of the computer game industry really took off, even faster than I had thought it would. At the same time, an independent game movement arose in opposition to this industrialization of the field. And this all happened at a time when the mass media were publishing sensationalized reports positioning computer games as a cultural menace (typically: they make people violent).
So for ALT+CTRL, we deliberately set out to showcase the independent game movement, especially those artists who took the position that games could be a positive force for social change, like any other art form. Not through propaganda but through its antidotes: informed criticality, expansive imagining, thoughtful tinkering, and original research. Where SHIFT-CTRL had been an invitation-only show, we organized ALT+CTRL as an open festival to draw in as wide and international a pool of artists as possible. Our one disappointment with this show is that we didn't get as many proposals from women as we wanted. On the other hand, I'm happy to say that we did have an early version of Auriea Harvey and Michaël Samyn's wonderful Tale of Tales in this show.

Did you grow up playing videogames? What is your personal relationship with this medium?
- I grew up playing all kinds of traditional games, especially those with strong elements of make-believe— Clue, Monopoly, Murder, Charades. But I was much more interested in books as a child, especially illustrated books. So I wasn't at all taken with the early computer games, which primarily rewarded speed of reflexes and rote learning of levels. I didn't find out about the Adventure-style text-based games until I was already involved with text-based RPGs.

The first computer game I really admired was the Myst/Riven series; I played that all the way through. I've played more MMORPGs than anything else, but much as I'm drawn to them I have huge issues with how they've become dominated by a self-reinforcing culture of viciousness that is most evident in the endless trash talk. The early RPGs were quite different in spirit, but you might not know that from the way the current discourse assumes people will 'always' behave badly in pseudonymous environments.

What is your take on the game and art connection, today? What is the role of digital gaming in our culture?
- Today I see computer games as just one (albeit commercially successful) form of playable media, along with user-driven installations, database art, simulation software, responsive robotics, and so on. The differences turn mainly on what kinds of rules are in place, how visible and constraining they are, and where the locus of power and control resides.
In my opinion, the most interesting areas of game development of the past few years are these:
• so-called 'serious games' that simulate aspects of our world as a form of experiential learning and/or user-centered research
• games that move away from the desktop mode, that rethink the relationship of interface, body, and place—e.g. Wii games, geocaching games
• alternate reality games and 'transmedia' games, with their blurring of boundaries between games and other forms of cultural production. (It's too bad that ARGs have so far been used almost exclusively as advertising by large corporations, but there's clearly a long way to go in the development of this format—most people still haven't even heard of them.)

What are you investigating these days, both as an artist and as a scholar?
- My own work has continued both to use gamelike, performative, and computational elements and to be about games as a cultural phenomenon. For instance, my 2008 performance project called Playing the Rapture was inspired by a really terrible computer

game about the Christian Rapture in which the player must battle the forces of the Antichrist in a post-Rapture world. In my piece, the plot revolves around two gamers who are creating and beta-testing a very similar game; their contests over and within this game are a proxy for their larger struggles over the necessity of rules and the problem of belief. I designed the environment for this piece to be almost entirely virtual—primarily large-scale projections of the game world the two gamers are testing. These projections were controlled through a pair of Max/MSP/Jitter patches that I wrote, and most of them were machinima videos that I created using the actual computer game, which was called Left Behind: Eternal Forces.

Another recent game-related project was World of World: The Adventures of Malbec and Player, commissioned in 2009 for a Laguna Museum show. It took the form of a 2 x 12-foot digital print that collaged screenshots from World of Warcraft with webcam images of a WoW player in his gaming den to create an implied narrative.

This project reflected my combined fascination and frustration with World of Warcraft, which I had been playing for several years at that point. In particular, it was a look at the relationship between players and avatars—a relationship that seems to me to be always troubled and generally oversimplified in writing about all kinds of virtual environments, not just that of WoW. The discourse around WoW has been very other-directed (e.g. how players behave towards other players, how they enact stereotypes), but what interests me is what we are doing to ourselves in virtual social environments like WoW. If avatars are sometimes less play than a form of self-enslavement and self-violation, what does that imply?

This piece reverses our usual perspective to consider the player through the avatar's eyes. It is as if a female Night Elf Death Knight (named Malbec) were looking back through the interface at the artificial (to her) world of the Player. In the way it encapsulates their joint experiences, it represents her view of him— and this is enhanced through an overlay of text fragments from an internal monologue in which she questions all aspects of their interaction.

The interview took place in October 2011.

Arne-Kjell Vikhagen: "Veøy" (2006)

Arne-Kjell Vikhagen is a Swedish artist and researcher at the University of Gothenburg. His PhD project investigates the artistic potential of computer game engines, specifically those engines used in first-person shooter games. A recent project of his - developed as a part of his dissertation - is a Game Art project called "Veøy", named after the island Veøy. Situated on the west coast of Norway, Veøy is a small island 0 measuring 1.1 square kilometres. Due to its former status as a former religious and trade centre, Veøy plays a special role for the local population. While doing research on the island. Vikhagen found an intriguing police report from 1934, where Arnulf Vikhagen claims to have seen "something unnatural" at Veøy.GameScenes talked to Vikhagen about his research project.

You are both an artist and an academic researcher. How would you describe the difference between Game Art in the Artworld and Game Art as an academic topic in Sweden today?
- There is, indeed, a difference, possibly because Game Art represents the incorporation of new technology in the fine arts. From an academic point of view, I think the interest is twofold: Firstly, new media art in general are still somewhat in the periphery of the fine arts sphere, but quite interesting for academics to study for the same reason. Secondly, it has become essential to understand the influence computer games on the contemporary aesthetics, especially if one is interested in understanding the 21st century visual culture. In my opinion, the Swedish art community is very adaptable and sensitive to new developments of contemporary art, even though it always will take some time before art made with new visual technologies find its way to agents, collectors, and museums.

The artwork "Veøy" plays a key part in your art and research, doesn't it?
-Yes, Veøy is the main project in my work, but also the most undefined. I suppose it's constantly a work in progress, as I am collecting material all the time. It has its starting point in an island

right next to where I grew up in Norway, that has all kinds of stories connected to it. I suppose that project is interesting for me because I get to mix folklore, archaeological research and local history with my own memories and thoughts on how much a place means for us. The island itself is a peculiar place – nobody lives there now, but it used to be the religious and commercial center of our fjord. The mix between what-has-been and here-and-now is intriguing, and I am looking forward to continue working with it in the years to come.

Why is the Unreal editor so popular among Game Artists?
- When I started working with Game Art, I tried a lot of different game engines before I landed on the Unreal Engine (the free runtime mostly, unless I do game mods). I still try other engines from time to time, and I really like some of the other open source engines, but I've sticked with the unreal engine for now. I like the way you can strip away the nice-looking surface, and keep the crude and primitive. That's important for me. I am not into fancy. When I worked with Veøy for instance, I obviously tried the Sandbox engine (FarCry), and it was great! It looked wonderful. So I had to go back to Unreal and make a polygon map of the island. It was a natural choice for me -- it didn't feel right. Maybe I'll change my mind about this in the future, if I find a way to combine the fancy with the primitive.

What strikes me about your Game Art projects is that they do not emphasize the notion of winning or losing: the "player" is often caught in a space or situation where he can not escape from as "To close for comfort" and "..and then you die". This theme is constant in your work...
- Yes, certainly. The works you mention are all concerned with that, and I think it's a pivotal topic for me. Not to say I have opinions about what happens when we die, because I really don't, but the outer periphery of human existence has fascinated me for quite some time, probably my whole life. The life/death symbolism in video games is so closely connected to the idea of progress, and as such is suits me perfectly. On a symbolic level, it connects the idea of progress and initiative to the fragile limits of our existence. Add

the aspect of morbid humour and you have a very strong combination for artistic expression!

The interview took place in November 2009.

Steve Manthorp: "Shooting Gallery" (2003)

To say that British artist Steve Manthorp (b. 1958) is "eclectic" would be an understatement. Manthorp's production ranges from woodcarving to Game Art. Curator of the Yorkshire Sculpture Park and Media Arts Officer, he collaborated with Shanaz Gulzar to create interactive digital artworks and public interventions. One of his most famous Game Art pieces is titled "Shooting Gallery" (2003 with Teddie Tapawan). Manthorp used the Unreal Engine to recreate an existing art gallery, specifically, the Cartwright Hall Art Gallery, as a digital, navigable space. This practice has become a staple in Game Art. In fact, one of the evergreen genres of Game Art is the playful subversion of "real" art spaces, like museums and galleries. Examples include Palle Torsson and Tobias Bernstrup's "Museum Meltdown" (1996), Orhan Kipcak "ArsDoom" (1993), and Hunter Jonakin "Jeff Koons Must Die!!!" (2011). Other Game Art projects include "Plasticity", a multiplayer urban planning game (with Mathias Fuchs, 2004), "EarthHeart" a serious game (With DESQ. Awarded R&D funding from MELT, 2006), "The Middleton Mystery", a serious game (commissioned by English Heritage for Belsay Hall, Northumberland, 2007 a "Time Gate" (2009), a game commission for Renaissance Knaresborough with Lateral Visions. In april of 2012, Mathias Jansson talked to Steve Manthorp talks to Steve Manthorp about his "mod(e)s of engagement" with the Artworld.

What is your relationship with video games?
- I have played computer games from their very earliest days. My first game purchase was a Binatone Ponggame which must have been in the mid-70s. It had four variants, all of which were almost identical. I still play computer games just as passionately. I'm currently playing Skyrim, Portal 2 & Amnesia on the PC and a couple of others on my Touchpad.

When did you begin to crate playful artistic interventions?
-In the late '70s and early '80s I was making kinetic sculpture, some of which were 'proto-videogames'; one in particular, Light Painting,

was a mechanical device which moved a luminous ball around within a cubic grid space – very crudely made, just a gantry & motorized bogey controlled with a home-made joystick. My first computer work was in the nineties, I guess, when I made a sculpture park in VRML. In the '80s I had been curator of the Yorkshire Sculpture Park; a job that made you all too aware of the physicality of sculpture.

Sitting a Henry Moore bronze, a Dordeigne stone carving or a Rickey mobile – and making it look as if God had dropped it there - was a major logistical undertaking. It was, I think, a reaction to that; to create a park in which the exhibits had no weight, no matter how large they were. Indeed, I remember that several of my exhibits floated in the air. I'm still interested in web 3D – one of my current websites, www.manthorp.co.uk was an early experiment in Lateral Vision's 3D web platform.

"Shooting Gallery" is one of your most famous artworks. For that piece, you re-created the Cartwright Hall Art Gallery inside Unreal. What were your goals, as an artist, but also as a game designer?

- "Shooting Gallery" was actually made in 2003, but became popular in 2004. I conceived the project as a marketing device for Cartwright Hall Art Gallery. The marketing officer there had undertaken some research among teenage boys and young men – a demographic that is extraordinarily hard to persuade into the art gallery – and had discovered that they didn't think galleries were 'for' them, or wanted them to be visitors. Furthermore, they were quite intimidated by these imposing, generally Victorian buildings with big wooden doors; they didn't know I what was on the other side of those doors.

I set out to design a project that would allow them to 'visit', familiarise themselves and even 'own' the art gallery before they had even set foot inside the real building. I knew this had to be on young people's own terms; you could build a thousand web 3D galleries and no kids would willingly choose to visit them: but give them the opportunity to deathmatch there and I guessed they would flock to it. It helped that Cartwright Hall was a perfect building for a small, tight UT deathmatch map. It was on three floors, had a wide open courtyard, two staircases and a lift. Sadly, the jump pad is an addition by the map designer. In the months after the map was released, you'd be amazed how many kids looked round behind the statue to see if it was there. At the time I was aware, of course, of other digital artists – 'computer artists', we were then – but oblivious to any working in the same area that I was.

How was "Shooting Gallery" made?
- A great part of the success of the project was the talent of the map's designer, Teddie Tapawan. He was an American, a passionate amateur UT map designer, one of whose maps was included in UT's official add-on map pack. He did a phenomenal job, just working with building plans and photographs. He's never visited Cartwright Hall, but the map is uncannily accurate & captures the feel of the building just as successfully as its architecture. As planet Unreal said at the time: 'This is one really unique, amazing looking map. So download it!'

The new map was a great success. Can you tell me about the response on the game?
- When it was released, it was given a double page spread and included on the cover DVDs of two of the leading UK games magazines which had supported the project. It was also covered by Edge and several national newspapers. Partly because of this good publicity, but mainly, I think, because it was a bloody good and very unusual map, downloads went through the roof. I can't remember the figures, but I think it had 13,700 downloads in the first three weeks, and that was just through the download sites we were monitoring.
We realised that we had a runaway success on our hands when the pornographers started using 'shooting gallery' and 'Cartwright Hall' as metatags on their home pages to dupe custom to their sites. It has been downloaded literally hundreds of thousands of times since its release. It's a great little map. It's still available from many different download sites. Just search for dm-cartwrighthall[fut] for

the original UT2003 map or DM-TDB-Cartwright Hall for the UT2004 update.

You have also created "PlastiCity", a multiplayer urban planning game with Mathias Fuchs. Can you tell me more about this project, the background and how it was done?
- One of the great regrets of my life is that we were not able to take PlastiCity beyond the proof of concept stage. I believe that the fully realised project would have been a genuinely useful tool in facilitating democratic engagement with the city planning process. Mathias and I had been introduced, I think, through a mutual friend. Mathias had been working on his pioneering project Expositur using the UT engine.

As soon as we met we started geeking out in the most hideous way and we knew we wanted to create a project together some time. Three Bradford Institutions - the National Media Museum, the University's School of Informatics and Bradford Council – were exploring the creation of a new collaborative creative industries crucible to be called Lightwave. They had some seed-corn funding and wanted to commission some exemplary content to iconise what a fully realised Lightwave institute might do.

We proposed a proof of concept pilot for PlastiCity. PlastiCity was a total conversion of UT which would allow local authorities to model their own city as a multiplayer environment and which provided a suite of tools to change every aspect of the urban environment. You could delete buildings, re-skin them, grow them, shrink them, replace them from a library of other buildings – there was even a 'listing gun' which prevented other players from changing a building for a period of time. You could 'green' areas, raise the water level, make pretty much any change you wanted. You could experience the city environment in a range of avatars, experiencing it from a buggy or a wheelchair to explore the implications of your decisions from a range of human perspectives.

The idea was that you would set up a multiplayer LAN in different community spaces and then populate it with city planners, urban architects and citizens; maybe even a few, brave, local politicians. We anticipated that there would be an hour of anarchy – great fun, but anarchy – but that after that, people would start conversing, using the toolset constructively and making collective decisions for the greater good. Unfortunately, the Lightwave project floundered for a number of reasons & we were unable to find the – relatively small – project funding to take the pilot to whole city centre scale. That is when it would have either proven itself to be a valuable tool or not. I'd love to revisit the idea with a more recent game engine. The principle is as valid now as it was then; equip city-makers and city-dwellers with a sandbox and the tools to explore ways of making their city a better place for living in.

How do you see on video games as an artistic tool and expression for future projects?
- I work mainly now as ADEPT in a co-practice with video artist Shanaz Gulzar. We work across the range of media arts and have made two videogames for heritage properties - The Middleton Mystery for English Heritage and Timegate for Knaresborough Castle, both with Carl Gavin & Lateral Visions. Games are powerful tools for what I call 'stealth education'. In a cunningly designed gamified environment, learning can be smuggled past players before they know what has hit them.

We believe that there would be a very exciting project in creating a real time ARG around a heritage property or number of heritage properties, with a narrative combining stealth education and tasks that would take the player around the sites. We're actively seeking a heritage trust partner for such an experiment. One of our key aims as artists is that we want to make work that does not compromise on quality and ambition, but which nonetheless appeals to the widest possible public. Games are engaging, immersive and fundamentally interactive artefacts which allow a particular, unique relationship between creator and player.

The game creator can guide and attempt to pre-guess the behaviour of the player, but can never determine how the player will navigate the game. Each player brings their own creative response to a playful environment. As a consequence, the artwork is to an extent a hybrid creation, experienced uniquely every time.

The interview took place in April 2012.

www.ingramcontent.com/pod-product-compliance
Lightning Source LLC
Chambersburg PA
CBHW020424220526
45464CB00002B/556